Irresponsible Citizenship

PETER LANG
PROMPT

PETER LANG
New York • Bern • Berlin
Brussels • Vienna • Oxford • Warsaw

Jean-François Caron

Irresponsible Citizenship

The Cultural Roots of the Crisis of Authority in Times of Pandemic

PETER LANG
New York • Bern • Berlin
Brussels • Vienna • Oxford • Warsaw

Library of Congress Cataloging-in-Publication Control Number: 2021022720

Bibliographic information published by **Die Deutsche Nationalbibliothek**.
Die Deutsche Nationalbibliothek lists this publication in the "Deutsche Nationalbibliografie"; detailed bibliographic data are available on the Internet at http://dnb.d-nb.de/.

ISBN 978-1-4331-8908-1 (hardcover)
ISBN 978-1-4331-8952-4 (ebook pdf)
ISBN 978-1-4331-8953-1 (epub)
ISBN 978-1-4331-8954-8 (mobi)
DOI 10.3726/b18495

This publication has been peer reviewed and meets the highest quality standards for content and production.

© 2021 Peter Lang Publishing, Inc., New York
80 Broad Street, 5th floor, New York, NY 10004
www.peterlang.com

All rights reserved.
Reprint or reproduction, even partially, in all forms such as microfilm, xerography, microfiche, microcard, and offset strictly prohibited.

Contents

Introduction 1
1. The Cultural Foundations of Disobedience and Conspiracy
   Theories 11
2. The Rights Revolution and the Evanescence of Authority 27
3. When Cultural Beliefs Challenge Respect for Political Authority 43
Conclusion: In Defence of Responsible Citizenship 67

Introduction

The COVID-19 pandemic has revealed how fragile the respect for political authority is in Liberal societies. Around the world, governments have encouraged their citizens to comply with very simple measures to limit the spread of the virus that has proven fatal to more than 3 million individuals (and counting): "wear a mask when you are outside your home and in the company of others," "stay at home and only go out if it is truly essential" and "avoid unnecessary gatherings" have been the most widespread instructions. However, although these instructions are more than reasonable given the presence of a virus that spreads from person to person through oral or nasal secretions, they have been ignored by a significant proportion of the world's population, thus contributing to the acceleration of the spread of the virus and even the development of a second and of a third wave of infections after initial freedom-restricting measures, such as the strict isolation of old and vulnerable persons in their places of residence, the quarantining of entire cities and even a ban on leaving one's home for any non-essential purpose, were implemented in many societies. This unwillingness of many people to follow the instructions of their respective governments has thus demonstrated just how relative and limited the power that the political sphere holds over citizens really is.

The following metaphor, taken from Michael Huemer (2013), illustrates the situation that liberal societies are now confronted with. Let us imagine the following scenario: you live in a neighbourhood where the peace and quiet is disturbed by a group of individuals who make excessive noise in the evenings, which prevents you from sleeping peacefully. Exasperated by this situation, you decide to take matters into your own hands. You therefore take a weapon and decide to arrest the individuals causing the problem, chaining them in your basement to teach them a lesson (obviously, you would make sure that they are properly fed). After a few weeks, you realize that your actions have paid off and that the neighbourhood is now peaceful. You then decide to pay your neighbours a visit to draw their attention to the newly quiet situation and, after they have explicitly acknowledged your statement, you tell them that you were responsible and they therefore owe you a financial contribution for your efforts—a contribution which, if not paid, will earn them a stay in your basement. There is no doubt that your neighbours will view this request as inappropriate and that they will consider your actions (with good reason) to actually be kidnapping, false imprisonment and extortion. In fact, they will unceremoniously send you away.

However, when you think about it, on the surface, your actions are nothing extraordinary in themselves, as they are very much in line with what governments do. In fact, your actions are similar in every way to the obligations of governments to enforce law and order and to arrest individuals who violate the rights of others. Requesting payment from your neighbours for services rendered to the community is similar to the requirement imposed by the state on all its citizens, namely, to pay their taxes or face the consequences if they refuse. However, whereas these actions are acceptable and necessary on the part of the state to guarantee respect for the social contract, peace, order and good governance, your militant or vigilante actions, on the other hand, would be eminently reprehensible.

In light of the current situation, this metaphor is particularly useful and reveals the attitude that some individuals have towards the directives imposed by various Western governments to prevent the spread of

COVID-19. For some, the decisions made by the state are similar to those of the self-proclaimed vigilante in our example. Like the neighbours confronted with your demands for payment, individuals who oppose state directives believe that the government is abusing its power, is illegitimate and is imposing arbitrary rules and punishments on others. Such an attitude is worrisome, to say the least, since a vigilante cannot be compared to a duly elected government. In a fundamental way, the thousands of individuals who thus openly question these decisions and call for civil disobedience no longer perceive the state to be legitimate, and they question its authority: a principle that requires, on the one hand, the recognition that the government has the right to impose rules that are deemed essential for groups to live together and, on the other hand, the obligation of citizens to respect those rules. When citizens question these premises, the state no longer exists, and the foundations of life together are threatened.

How and why did we get here? This is a question that should be haunting everyone. This refusal to obey what some people perceive to be a "vigilante state" is not limited to the obligatory wearing of a mask or social distancing. I am of the opinion that the COVID-19 crisis has revealed the cultural crisis of liberal societies that have been following a path over the last decade that can explain people's careless and irresponsible behaviours demonstrating their lack of respect for the authority of the state. There are many reasons to fear the decay of the overarching sense of attachment people feel towards their country. During this pandemic, the unwillingness to follow governments' directives has prevented the flattening of the curve of contamination, thus contributing to the increase in the number of infected individuals; therefore, we need to think beyond the current situation and consider what the other ramifications of the erosion of respect for political authority could be. What we have seen could simply be only the tip of the iceberg of the future problems this situation may bring us. Indeed, when political authority is not respected or when it is challenged by other feelings of attachment (whether individualistic or collective), societies lose their perennial meaning. They are no longer able to unite millions of strangers together and ask them to make sacrifices for each other. When such a situation prevails, societies are at the mercy of selfish, anti-social and hyper-individualistic behaviours or are plagued by sub-national clusters of belonging that recall the medieval period, when identity and solidarity were fragmented. Liberal societies are to be blamed for that erosion of centralized political authority. Why is this so?

First and foremost, this health crisis has exposed the popularity of conspiracy theories in Western societies and the growing mistrust people have in governments. For example, several surveys have shown that a significant number of individuals believe that there is a connection between the virus and 5G antennas or even that there is a widespread conspiracy to force individuals to be vaccinated so that they can be better controlled. The popularity of these theories seems to be associated with various factors, including the social exclusion or low income or educational level of its supporters. In fact, when individuals who already find themselves in a difficult situation see that their position is becoming even more precarious as a result of an event with as significant an impact as that of COVID-19, any form of explanation—even the most far-fetched—offers these individuals a form of reassurance. However, this quest for meaning actually hides a much deeper evil that is unique to our modern world, the foundations of which have been strongly influenced by science so that natural phenomena cannot be accepted as the result of mere contingencies. In contrast, the predominant belief is that everything that happens to us can have only a rational explanation; thus, the possibility that a phenomenon could have a very simple explanation is unfamiliar in our consciousness. In other words, far from being the result of a dysfunction of reason, these conspiracy theories are rather the sign of the over-rationalization of a phenomenon, and this novel coronavirus is a good example in this regard. Most likely the result of close contact between humans and exotic animals in a market in Wuhan, China, this respiratory virus has rapidly spread everywhere across the globe through a process similar to the spread of the common cold or flu. However, given its global repercussions, reminiscent of the frightening time of the plague or Spanish flu, this explanation is far too simple and dubious to many people. The impact and complexity of the virus, the nature of which has long eluded the best epidemiologists on the planet, cannot be the result of such an eventuality, according to these sceptical individuals. We have come to believe that nature is not unfathomable; thus, this virus that has forced us to dramatically alter our way of life requires an explanation as complex as the virus itself and the identification of its true cause. Not surprisingly, the state and its representatives are the main victims of this scientific legacy, since the entire liberal political system is based on the principle of intersubjective mistrust. Consequently, when the unexplained befalls us, many people's natural reflex is to enhance the coherence of this phenomenon by assigning a culprit—the state and its representatives being the obvious suspects—as well as an apparently structured explanation: a process that leads to conspiracy theories. As such, when a significant part of the population believes in these delusional theories, it is hardly surprising that tension arises between their supporters and the directives emanating from the state. Obedience then gives way to distrust and, ultimately, to defiance. Society therefore needs to once again embrace contingencies and the unexplained.

Second, for more than half a century, Liberal societies have taken a dangerously libertarian course, the consequence of which has been the upsetting of the necessary balance between the enjoyment of one's individual freedom and the reasonable restrictions to which that same freedom must be subjected. As a result of the "rights revolution" of the 1960s, this drift has generated a mentality in which individual fulfilment, self-realization and the desire for authenticity predominate. These principles are not problematic in and of themselves. In contrast, they are even to be celebrated to the extent that it is difficult to imagine rational individuals who would accept that their behaviours or their idea of a good life can be dictated by others. Individual freedom—or "negative freedom," as it is also known—is a goal that everyone should aspire to. This ideal should not be called into question. However, where the problem arises is when this libertarian enjoyment occurs at the expense of the collective interest, and unfortunately, today's liberal societies have fallen into this spiral. In fact, I would go so far as to assert that the expression "liberal society" has become an oxymoron insofar as contemporary liberalism has long since caused the meaning and scope of the intersubjective links that serve precisely to "create society" to disappear. Although individualism is fundamental in any society that values it, the men and women making up that society are nevertheless still required to project themselves collectively within that same communal destiny, failing which, social belonging would be nothing more than mere rational calculations by individuals who seek only to maximize their own interests by moving constantly and without any scruples from one relationship to another. When this sense of belonging to a world that is beyond our reach and based on which we should assess the value of our individual choices is lacking, there is no longer a society, only communities of egoists with a destiny that lasts only as long as the agreement of its members on a momentary common interest. In many ways, this theoretical description corresponds to the face of today's liberal societies: a face that has become apparent during the COVID-19 crisis, as many citizens have deliberately chosen to ignore health rules to enjoy their freedom to the detriment of others' health. Worse still, when faced with state-imposed measures to reduce cases of infection, many individuals openly opted for civil disobedience, arguing that these measures infringe on their individual freedoms.

Last, the COVID-19 crisis has also revealed that cultural and religious beliefs have offset state directives to ensure social distancing. Indeed, in many cases, people have given more weight to these convictions and have knowingly chosen to ignore public laws or decrees, which has contributed to the spread of the virus. Although we cannot deny the importance of recognizing and respecting these beliefs, this crisis has nonetheless shown that they may be detrimental to the common good when people's inclination to respect them prevail over the necessity of respecting public norms. This is worrying in the sense that liberal societies have been following a model over the last 40 years that runs the risk of making this reality increasingly common in the future. As a result of their willingness to promote people's right to be authentic without having to fear any form of interference or discrimination (an approach that is directly responsible for the problem evoked above), modern societies have also promoted the necessity of recognizing and accommodating every minority group present in a given society. This policy of multiculturalism has therefore valued sub-national identities (whether they are ethnic, cultural or religious). If this idea is good in itself and not to be questioned in principle, its application has nonetheless led to the consolidation of identities that are now competing against the broader and overarching identity of the state. This quest for recognition and accommodation has therefore resulted in communitarian clusters that, if pursued, run the risk of generalizing in the future what has been seen during this crisis, namely, cultural or religious beliefs that lead individuals to behave and act contrary to state directives.

***

This pandemic has allowed us to observe the extent to which the crisis affects political authority, and it must therefore lead us to reflect in depth on its causes and ways to correct the situation. Obviously, the imbalance that has arisen in favour of an excessive and irresponsible enjoyment of individual freedom should not lead us to consider the other extreme as a solution, namely, the strict and repressive regulation thereof. In this respect, the success of the Chinese model, which (at least according to the official version) was able to contain the resurgence of a second and a third wave, cannot serve as a model to be followed. As I said before, individual freedom is a value that human societies must cherish and value: an idea that is totally foreign to that totalitarian regime. The reader must be aware that despite all its current flaws, liberal ideology ought to be preserved. Instead of sacrificing such ideology and seeing it as unfit to face serious situations such as a pandemic, the goal is rather to create a better balance between negative freedom and the necessary civic-mindedness that must drive all citizens. Far from being an attack on individual freedom, achieving this happy medium is, on the contrary, the most effective guarantee against a possible violation of individual rights. In fact, individuals must understand that their inability to strike the right balance, as manifested in the pre-eminence given to the enjoyment of their individual freedom at the expense of the interests of the community, opens the door to the infringement of that same freedom.

This paradox can easily be explained. Faced with such individualistic behaviour, those individuals who are compliant with health rules have naturally condemned actions that are potentially detrimental to the health of others. These individuals have rightly viewed such actions as a dangerous attack on the public interest. As a consequence, this has led to growing calls for stricter measures worthy of a police state or authoritarian regime. Such calls are quite understandable from a public health perspective, but they are also symptomatic of a broader need for political authority along with an awareness of the excesses and dangers of the individualist theory. In times of crisis, paradoxically, followers of the liberal approach seem to call for the return of strict authority. In a reversal reminiscent of the legend of Dostoyevsky's Grand Inquisitor, individuals who have been granted freedom end up becoming aware of its excesses and the insecurity it causes. Faced with the anarchy that often accompanies periods of crisis, the population demands more authority, sometimes to the point of advocating extreme forms of control. Worn down by anxiety (the somewhat Hobbesian fear of dying under atrocious conditions from a virus), the population willingly accepts being guided and reassured by all means, even if it means permanently giving up some of its freedom.

This is exactly the threat currently looming over the Western model of governance. We are reminded of the warnings of Benjamin Constant and Alexis de Tocqueville that the abuse of negative freedom can lead to tyranny. In this case, the erosion of authority partly due to this same phenomenon could lead to similar consequences. It is not a question of eventually sacrificing the entirety of the founding principles of liberalism but rather of the containment of liberalism to prevent such abuses as we are currently seeing. It would be a mistake to respond disproportionately to the criminal individualistic behaviour revealed by the crisis, as this could result in policies that would bring about lasting structural change and take liberal societies down a dangerously slippery slope. In regard to the protection of people's natural rights, a spirit of moderation ought to prevail.

In the same vein, the fact that cultural beliefs have derailed states' efforts to limit the spread of the virus, the recognition of the value of minority cultures should not be questioned as a consequence. Indeed, cultures play a fundamental role in people's capacities to make choices and value their respective conception of what constitutes a good life, which is why discrimination needs to be fought and why forcing ethnocultural minorities to assimilate into a single societal cultural world causes terrible prejudices. In this regard, the objective is rather to determine how to provide the expected recognition of the beliefs of ethnocultural or religious minorities in a way that will nonetheless keep their categorical importance subordinated to the overall good of society when the situation dictates the necessity of doing so.

If the COVID-19 pandemic has shown that liberal societies are defined by a form of irresponsible citizenship and a lack of respect for political authority, it has also provided us with the capacity to identify the sources of this crisis, which allows us to find a fitting remedy. However, this remedy implies finding a better balance between the necessary liberty we ought to give to people and the necessity of them abiding by states' directives when needed. Finding this balance is very difficult, as it would be very easy to suggest mechanisms that would ultimately lead to the subordination of people to the interests of the state. This option should never prevail, as preserving individual freedom ought to be the chief objective of modern societies. What needs to be done, however, is figuring out how to lead people to use their personal liberty in a responsible fashion. This is the task I set myself in this book, which is a logical extension of arguments I have previously developed and argued elsewhere (Caron 2020abc, 2021).

References

Caron, Jean-François. *A Sketch of the World After the Covid-19 Crisis: Essays on Political Authority, The Future of Globalization and the Rise of China*. London: Palgrave MacMillan, 2020a.

———. "Le meilleur régime politique en temps de pandémie." *La Presse*, March 16, 2020b.

———. "Quand l'État devient un justicier illégitime." *Le Devoir*, November 7, 2020c.

———. "Entre coercition et dissuasion : la crise de l'autorité." *Le Devoir*, January 23, 2021.

Huemer, Michael. *The Problem of Political Authority: An Examination of the Right to Coerce and the Duty to Obey*. London: Palgrave MacMillan, 2013.

Chapter One

The Cultural Foundations of Disobedience and Conspiracy Theories

"5G technology is related to COVID-19," "It is a way for Bill Gates to implant digital microchips that will control people once they receive the vaccine," "COVID-19 does not really exist and is simply a way for political elites to take away our freedom." Everybody has heard at least one of these assertions since the beginning of the COVID-19 crisis. Indeed, polls have found that 29% of Americans believe the virus was made in a lab (Pew Research Center 2020), 19% of Americans believe that this virus is part of an orchestrated depopulation plan by the United Nations or the New World Order, and 23% believe that it is either definitely or probably true that the vaccine will deliberately infect people with a poison (Boyle 2020). It is possible to observe similar trends elsewhere. A study published in October 2020 showed that 22% of respondents in Great Britain found the claim that COVID-19 was engineered in a Wuhan laboratory reliable. The percentage rose to 26% in Ireland, 33% in Mexico and 37% in Spain. It also showed that 22% of people in Mexico, 18% in Ireland and Spain thought that COVID-19 was part of a plot to force global vaccination, while 16% in Mexico and Spain, 12% in Ireland and 8% in Great Britain believed that 5G was somehow connected with the virus

(Roozenbeek et al. 2020). Needless to say, such beliefs have tremendous consequences on the rest of society as well as on their believers. Indeed, when these beliefs lead countless individuals to disregard government directives in times of a pandemic, they directly contribute to accelerating the spread of the virus, which can then infect individuals who have made the decision to abide by the rules.

What can explain such attitudes that have led many in Western societies to actively disobey state directives by refusing to wear a mask in public, by organizing mass events at a time when individuals are asked to limit their contact or by committing arsonous attacks on telecommunication towers? Many causes explaining the existence of conspiracy theories have already been discussed in psychology. First, these theories serve an epistemic function, as they are able to provide what appears to be a coherent explanation that helps preserve individuals' most sincere beliefs (for instance, that vaccines are inherently dangerous, that 9/11 was staged by the CIA or that climate change is a hoax) and understanding of the world at a time when societies are facing large or significant challenges (Leman and Cinnirella 2013, Lewandowsky et al. 2013). Studies have indeed shown that the incentive to turn towards these theories is higher when a situation leaves people anxious and powerless (Grzesiak-Feldman 2013). This mechanism is easily understandable, as the need to find meaning when chaos prevails is a fundamental characteristic of human minds and allows people to regulate their trauma and find a necessary sense of well-being (Graeupner and Coman 2017, 218). Conspiracy theories are very effective in this regard because they are resistant to any form of falsification, as they can easily adapt to contradictions thanks to their capacity to find favourable new evidence or because those who attack them are often depicted as being part of the very conspiracy the theory is describing. For example, I remember that at the beginning of the second wave of COVID-19 infections, many proponents of these beliefs went into hospitals to record themselves with their smartphones in order to demonstrate the absence of patients and to prove that the government was lying and making up infection numbers. However, when cases started to rise once again, the same individuals justified the flood of hospital emergencies by stating that the government had purposely infected people. The fact of the matter is that it is simply impossible to win a discussion with an adherent of such theories: they will always be right no matter how hard authorities try to prove them wrong.

This being said, the question I am interested in is how liberal societies are designed in a way that fosters these beliefs. Of course, I am not suggesting that such societies are responsible for the presence of these theories, which have always been present historically and in every type of society. This would be a foolish assumption and would ignore that conspiracy theories that led to the massacre of Jews during the medieval period because they were—as it was said at the time—planning to poison water wells or that of women in Salem who were burnt alive for purportedly conspiring with the devil. We could also mention *the Protocols of the Elders of Zion*, which have played a significant role in fostering antisemitism. African and South American ethnographies have also shown the presence of these beliefs in rural areas, as individuals are often accused of witchcraft when a calamity is affecting local inhabitants (van Prooijen and Douglas 2018, 899). Even if this phenomenon is universal, there are nonetheless factors specific to liberal societies that can explain why this social trend is on the rise.

The fact that freedom of expression and tolerance towards unsettling ideas—even the most eccentric ones—are cornerstones of liberal societies certainly explains their prevalence, which is now reinforced by the presence of the internet and social media that allow conspiracy theorists to openly express themselves and share their beliefs and, consequently, to reach out to millions of other individuals. This combination of factors has helped misguided and fake interpretations of reality that were previously private to gain a place in the public discourse. For the first time in history, individuals now have access at a very low cost—with only a single click—to countless ideas, beliefs and theories that can shape their realities. On the other hand, the availability of this information comes with a price: the possibility that much of this information may simply be pure invention and we therefore lack the capacity to verify its accuracy. This creates a vicious circle. Indeed, the vast majority of individuals are not open to opportunities to disconfirm their beliefs. Again, this is perfectly understandable, since we need to be able to draw meaning from the complex realities around us, which implies the necessity of grounding it in solid foundations that are not liable to crumble at the first sign of contradiction. The dialectical method may unfortunately be discomforting for too many of us. As a result, an internet user can easily find a variety of online sources that confirm his most sincere beliefs even if they have no validity whatsoever, because individuals show a tendency to only consult sources that confirm what they already think. In this sense, we are far from seeing the emergence of a global community of knowledge thanks to our contemporary technological revolution that resembles the one following Johannes Gutenberg's invention of the printing press in the 15th century. Rather than seeing the internet and the proliferation of information tools as sources of enlightenment that might finally set the ground for a new political agora that would place the citizen at the centre of the decision-making process, we should view these developments critically and as factors that increase people's gullibility. This process is further reinforced by online search histories that will, thanks to algorithms, orient users to other websites and sources that will also confirm what they already think. People will therefore have the impression that they have achieved scientific certainty about a fact as the result of a rigorous investigation. Paradoxically, the unprecedented access to knowledge that the internet provides has proven itself to be a powerful tool of ignorance. At the end of the day, this is the real perniciousness of conspiracy theories: they can drive people away from obeying their government and respecting its authority, as the COVID-19 crisis has shown. Indeed, all social psychology studies have made it clear that proponents of conspiracy theories commonly accuse governmental institutions—whether politicians in general or state agencies and sectors that are connected with the state because of the services they are providing, such as pharmaceutical companies—of plotting against them (van Prooijen and Douglas 2018).

I think it is fair to say that the internet and social media are not destined to disappear anytime soon. On the contrary, they are definitely here to stay. Thus, the desire to regulate them appears to be the only available option and seems to be quite feasible. However, this option still comes with numerous questions related to the way it ought to be done. Indeed, who should determine the regulations—the corporations themselves or statesmen? What should the criteria be for determining what kind of information should be banned or remain available? Although an overwhelming majority of conspiracy theories have historically revealed themselves to be unfounded, a few have actually been proven true. The best example is probably the Watergate scandal, which was at first ridiculed by the Nixon administration and its supporters before journalists Carl Bernstein and Bob Woodward provided clear evidence that the Republicans had spied on their Democrat rivals. In this sense, any form of censorship runs the risk of silencing the truth. What needs to be avoided is thus the imposition of a single narrative and the silencing of diverging points of view under the pretext that they are false. There is an inherent risk for liberal states that they will end up following an authoritarian path by trying to regulate access to information. The question of how to combat such theories therefore remains unanswered.

However, what I wish to emphasize in this chapter is how easy and widely available access to information interacts with other fundamental features of liberal societies to further increase people's mistrust in their governments. In other words, broader access to information does not automatically correlate with a growing tendency of people to start doubting those in positions of authority. It is rather associated with the historical and cultural context of liberalism as a philosophical tradition that has made central to our understanding of the world concepts that can fuel a lack of respect for authority. The valorization of freedom of expression is one factor that can explain the popularity of conspiracy theories in liberal societies; likewise, the principle of equality also plays a pivotal role in this regard, as it tends to deprive experts of their status. As I have already argued elsewhere, liberalism celebrates the idea of equality between men and women almost as a religious dogma (Caron 2020, 5–21). As a consequence, people tend to refuse any form of authority placed over them, as this is seen as an unwelcome form of infantilization that denies their right to equality. This phenomenon has been made possible thanks to the recent technological revolution. Easy access to forms of knowledge that were once unavailable or that required time and effort to obtain is indeed allowing non-experts to compete with doctors and scientists for attention in public discourse.

Indeed, there is a direct correlation between individuals having the impression that they are knowledgeable about a specific question and the same individuals having a lack of trust in those who are actually experts in the field (Bronner 2013, 395). In other words, the more people tend to consider themselves informed about a scientific question, the more they will doubt scientists: a situation that greatly resembles what Plato described in Phaedrus regarding a philosophy of education based on memorizing knowledge:

> The specific which you have discovered is an aid not to memory, but to reminiscence, and you give your disciples not truth, but only the semblance of truth; they will be hearers of many things and will have learned nothing; they will appear to be omniscient and will generally know nothing; they will be tiresome company, having the show of wisdom without the reality. (Plato, Phaedrus, par. 275a)

This issue, combined with the fact that those who are giving advice on how to behave are defined as part of the conspiracy, produces a context in which everybody starts thinking that their personal "knowledge" is of equal value to that of experts: a principle reinforced by the notion of equality between people that will be discussed in the next chapter. As a result, authority figures tend to lose their capacity to influence and control others. Therefore, it is fundamental that individuals not automatically see other people's knowledge as strictly equal to theirs but that individuals recognize that experts are the bearers of a social status that they have acquired through time and effort. Accepting this subordination is by no means an infringement upon or a denial of their capacity to benefit from equal treatment, as they remain the bearer of the same rights and obligations as those who have acquired specific knowledge. This is why students must accept that the person standing in front of them delivering a lecture and grading their papers is a professor to whom their owe respect and deference. Similarly, individuals watching a TV program in which a scientist discusses the measures that should be implemented to fight a deadly virus need to acknowledge that the scientist's expertise warrants that her advice ought to be followed. When people start losing this capacity to see others as a social group's normal representatives whose expertise should not be challenged in the name of equality, authority collapses. Thus, disobedience, rebellion, and an absence of deference are not social foundations upon which societies can be built.[1]

The idea that traditional figures of authority have lost their capacity to influence people's lives, either because they are thought to be part of a conspiracy or because our knowledge is now as valuable as theirs thanks to our enhanced capacity to access information that was once reserved to these groups and our twisted interpretation of equality, does not explain everything. It is also a constitutive element of the modernist philosophical legacy of the last 300 years that was built, in part, upon the necessity of doubting institutions and figures of authority due to their propensity to deny people the capacity to independently determine their actions and their respective conceptions of what constitutes a good life. The most famous call in this regard remains that by Immanuel Kant against the "guardians" that have kept us chained to dogmas and beliefs that keep human beings in a state of mental slavery and thus prevents people from leading their lives according to their own reasoning (Kant 1784). Liberating humans from the various chains that have prevented them from enjoying their freedom has been the quest of modern liberal societies, and people have therefore been

---

[1] When this is the case, societies begin to feel what Plato described in *The Republic* (562c–563d). A similar pattern was once observed by Plato in his criticism about democracy. While people should listen to those with relevant knowledge, they would rather pay attention to individuals who are only pretending to have such knowledge, thereby leading the democratic city to decay. In his famous comparison of a sick man and a physician, Plato wrote the following: "On several occasions I have been with my brother Herodicus or some other physician to see one of his patients, who would not allow the physician to give him medicine, or apply a knife or hot iron to him; and I have persuaded him to do for me what he would not do for the physician just by the use of rhetoric. And I say that if a rhetorician and a physician were to go to any city, and had there to argue in the Ecclesia or any other assembly as to which of them should be elected state-physician, the physician would have no chance; but he who could speak would be chosen if he wished; and in a contest with a man of any other profession the rhetorician more than anyone would have the power of getting himself chosen, for he can speak more persuasively to the multitude than any of them, and on any subject. Such is the nature and power of the art of rhetoric" (*Gorgias*, 456bc).

encouraged to doubt all types of authorities that have tried to restrain their actions. Indeed, for Kant, modernity

> is the genuine age of criticism, to which everything must submit. Religion through its holiness and legislation through its majesty commonly seek to exempt themselves from it. But in this way they excite a just suspicion against themselves, and cannot lay claim to that unfeigned respect that reason grants only to that which has been able to withstand its free and public examination. (Kant 1998, 100–101)

As a result, this tradition that combines the idea of equality between individuals with the necessity of doubting authority has created an explosive cocktail leading to a deep crisis of authority in modern liberal societies. In such circumstances, states are left with two options, both of which are thought to be replacements of authority, namely, the use of coercive measures by the state or resorting to an equalitarian dialogical process that is aimed at convincing individuals to follow a certain path. These are the options that have been privileged by liberal societies during the COVID pandemic, and they have proven their limits, which is why they should not be considered effective solutions for encouraging people's obedience. Later in this essay, I will provide a thorough explanation of why we should be wary of these alternatives, but for the time being, I will simply say that genuine authority relies upon a natural inclination of people to obey individuals who have acquired a higher social standing through their virtues and talents. In contrast, as has been argued by Hannah Arendt, obedience and respect for authority have failed whenever they rely upon force and violence or when their efficiency is dependent upon persuasion. As I will discuss later on, a responsible form of citizenship requires other foundations for authority.

The COVID crisis has clearly revealed to us the deep cultural crisis of liberal societies and the vicious circle in which they are trapped. When political leaders and scientists have to explain *ad nauseam* in press conferences or on television the logic behind the necessity of wearing masks, practicing social distancing and avoiding unnecessary travel as the prime way of convincing the populace to abide by the rules, they are simply proving their failure to generate authority. In return, this generates a counter-reaction on the part of irresponsible individuals who, in the name of equality and their obligation to exercise doubt regarding the leaders who are merely interested in keeping them docile, provide "evidence" that their government is either abusing its power or lying to them. Faced with this situation, the government will have no other choice but to impose liberticidal measures primarily aimed at forcing these defiant citizens to obey. These normally last-resort coercive measures that are being adopted illustrates like no other example the decline in governmental authority. Ultimately, this is a zero-sum game that can only lead societies on a slippery slope since this violence will further increase the resentment of those refusing to abide by their state's rules and reinforce the schism between them and the state's leaders, thereby creating a political environment that is conducive to populism—a current that, as we have unfortunately witnessed under the Trump presidency, exponentially accelerates the erosion of authority.

Moreover, there is another fundamental component of liberalism that further increases this lack of trust in government and fuels the popularity of conspiracy theories, namely, the fact that trust in public authorities is based on an institutionalization of mistrust. Indeed, the liberal tradition has been built upon the idea that societies ought to serve humans' needs and goals and not the other way around. This value given to individualism has created a system in which people believe they ought to be given the greatest room to enjoy their private freedom, which has been called "negative freedom".[2] This belief implies that there is no obligation on the part of individuals to be involved in politics if doing so does not correspond to their own idea of happiness. This can obviously be very problematic, as obsession with only one's own affairs may ultimately be detrimental to one's interests in the long run. Indeed, as warned by various liberal authors, such as Benjamin Constant and Alexis de Tocqueville, choosing to ignore what those in charge of protecting our natural rights are doing comes at the risk of

---

2   Of course, people's negative freedom is not absolute and can be limited upon reasonable grounds in a free and democratic society, especially if their actions will have a negative impact on another person's life or capacity to pursue happiness.

having those rights be violated and seeing the emergence soft despotism. The best metaphor in this regard is probably the one from Constant in which he compares the representative system of government with the feeling of rich individuals that they need to hire an accountant to help them manage their finances. He writes:

> The representative system is nothing but an organization by means of which a nation charges a few individuals to do what it cannot or does not wish to do herself. Poor men look after their own business; rich men hire stewards. (…) the representative system is a proxy given to a certain number of men by the mass of the people who wish their interests to be defended and who nevertheless do not have the time to defend themselves. But, unless they are idiots, rich men who employ stewards keep a close watch on whether these stewards are doing their duty, lest they should prove negligent, corruptible, or incapable; and, in order to judge the management of these proxies, the landowners, if they are prudent, keep themselves well-informed about affairs, the management of which they entrust to them. Similarly, the people who, in order to enjoy the liberty which suits them, resort to the representative system, must exercise an active and constant surveillance over their representatives, and reserve for themselves, at times which should not be separated by too lengthy intervals, the right to discard them if they betray their trust, and to revoke the powers which they might have abused. (Constant 1988, 325–26)

The opinion on how individuals in modern societies ought to preserve their liberties is unambiguous in this quote: "surveillance," "betrayed trust" and "abuse of power" are the basis of the dynamic between citizens and their leaders, which is defined by a fundamental absence of trust. This lack of confidence has generally led to the development of institutions and mechanisms that have made distrust their core defining notion, such as counter-powers, constant auditing and, in some cases, a recall process that can lead to the dismissal of elected officials. As predicted in Machiavelli's dark assessment of human nature (Caron 2019, 23–32), modern societies are therefore established on the idea that we cannot trust individuals with power and that those who are enjoying it will never hesitate to abuse it if they are given the chance to do so. This view is reserved not only for political leaders but also for many professions whose members' professionalism is guaranteed through the strict deontological codes that hang over their heads like the sword of Damocles. Consequently, this institutionalized logic of deep mistrust between normal individuals and those who are in a position of authority over them also helps explain the popularity of conspiracy theories involving politicians and those whom they work closely with. Thus, it is not surprising that those who are most inclined to agree with conspiracy theories are individuals who already have reason to mistrust the government because of their stigmatized or disadvantaged social position and may have come to believe that the elite have rigged the system against them (Crocker et al. 1999, Imhoff and Bruder 2014).

Another factor playing a role in the growing trend of conspiracy theories in modern liberal societies is the fact that the erosion of traditional beliefs has led to the right to doubt, which has also triggered another unique phenomenon, namely, the need to determine the reasons behind every situation an individual or society encounters. With the dominance of reason, there is no space for error or the irrationality of humans as potential explanations when contingencies strike. In the world of Western democracies, people have been told and trained to believe over the last 300 years that every phenomenon has a rational explanation and that nothing is merely the fruit of fate. There is indeed a visceral need to understand in a scientific manner all incidents; it is as if our minds can no longer be satisfied with explanations that rely on fate. The use of reason in a rigorous scientific manner provides a necessary comfort to many of us who, faced with the loss of religious transcendence as a coping mechanism, need a new way to make sense of the events we are facing. This can only be achieved in an anthropocentric way.

We cannot ignore how effective religion has been in making sense of the contingencies that the human race has had to face in the past and in explaining why the world is so unjust and difficult to live in. Indeed, we need to understand why some children are born with serious physical or intellectual deficiencies; why, for example, a 3-year-old child must suffer from an incurable brain tumour; or why hard-working individuals who have a strong work ethic may nonetheless fail in their attempt to start a company, while less talented and dedicated individuals succeed in their projects. Be it through the messianic eschatology of a God who will re-establish justice after the end of days or through the

Indian doctrine of karma, religions are able to provide us with a way to understand what does not appear to make sense. With the "death of God," *ersatz* explanations had to be found. In some cases, reason and scientific reasoning have fulfilled this role, as have ideological systems such as fascism and communism, which took over as secular religions by offering to their followers a complex set of explanations about all of humankind's deep metaphysical questions about the fate of society, the sense of history and the meaning of major political events.

Providing evidence-based explanations to all contingencies is obviously an imperfect way of assessing reality, as individuals do, whether we like it or not, take irrational actions that are difficult to explain. As a result, this process of over-reasoning about everything opens the door to the development of conspiracy theories because of their capacity to make sense of the inexplicable. Since nothing is due to luck, everything must have an explanation, and these theories provide just that by taking advantage of the profound mistrust people have of their governments. Many examples come to mind, including the tragic 2010 earthquake in Haiti that caused the death of more than 200,000 people. This terrible event that affected the poorest country in the Americas could hardly have been foreseen, as this part of *fortuna* evades human control. But this was not the opinion of everyone who could not accept fate as the reason for this human tragedy. In the days that followed, people tried to "make sense" of the event by developing a conspiracy theory that was based upon the idea that the United States had caused the earthquake using a seismic device developed through the High-frequency Active Auroral Research Program (HAARP) to trigger the earthquake by sending ultrasound waves through the water towards Port-au-Prince. Conspiracists pointed to the strange activities previously conducted by the U.S. Navy in the region and to the fact that having a U.S.-friendly government in Haiti is geopolitically relevant to the U.S. government. The earthquake was therefore an opportunity that allowed the U.S. to regain the upper hand in Haiti country by taking a lead in giving humanitarian aid to the country.

The same can be said regarding the 9/11 terrorist attacks, whose barbarian and indiscriminate nature were beyond comprehension to the common individual. Indeed, is it even possible to make sense of using commercial airliners filled with innocent people and transforming them into flying bombs to destroy buildings full of other individuals who, outside the irrational accusations of terrorists, have done nothing wrong? Again, many of us needed to make sense of that fateful day. It is therefore not surprising that other possible explanations were developed and spread all over the world thanks to the internet. Rather than blaming irrational al Qaeda operatives, conspiracy theorists provided what they saw as a logical explanation armed with scientific evidence: this event had been planned by the U.S. government. According to the conspiracy theorists, the way the Twin Towers collapsed evidences the use of controlled demolitions using explosives that had been installed in the buildings beforehand. Other conspiracists developed a "no-plane theory," arguing that missiles surrounded by holograms made them look like planes and noting that an object seen underneath the planes' fuselages is missing from normal Boeing 767s. The list goes on. For these people, 9/11 was a false flag operation necessary to trigger a new defence policy aimed at transforming the U.S. into a global hegemon. Furthermore, it allowed the U.S. to justify new wars abroad as a way to establish a solid presence in the Middle East and Central Asia to guarantee the supply of oil and natural gas in the decades to come and, consequently, to hinder Russia and China's strategic interests, as depicted in the widely known documentary *The Oil Factor: Behind the War on Terror.* The documentary argues that the invasions of Afghanistan and Iraq fit into a coherent historical trend of the United States seeking to establish military bases in countries to allow it to control 90% of global energy resources.

It is possible to think of many other similar examples. Despite their differences, they all share the same fundamental features, namely, a purportedly scientific and rational appraisal based on what is thought to be evidence. Therefore, believing in conspiracy theories is by no means a sign of the malfunctioning of people's reason, of their madness or of their loss of touch with reality. It is rather an indicator of a typical modern mindset that gives precedence to the right to doubt and the use of reason as the only way to understand and explain the world that surrounds us—a process reinforced by the institutional mechanisms of distrust that are inherently connected with the value liberalism grants to political participation. These elements provide the necessary elements for the establishment of a conspiracy mindset that provides the illusion of explanatory depth.

Conclusion

This short discussion on how the culture of doubt and of disobedience towards governments is intimately connected with the cultural and philosophical foundations of liberal Western societies is only a small taste of the broader negative implications of the main pillars in such societies of respect for political authority. This is because the supremacy of the principles of equality of all humankind and of the value of negative freedom over any other considerations has also limited the deference to those in charge in other ways. As I will explain in the next chapter, this phenomenon is due in large part to the "rights revolution" that first emerged in the 1960s and has exponentially accelerated the individualistic and egalitarian seeds that were planted some 300 years ago. However, as the COVID-19 crisis has shown us, the extreme expressions of this revolution come with the risk of a liberticidal reaction on the part of the state that individuals ought to be aware of.

References

Boyle, Louise. "US Election Poll: One in Five Believe Covid-19 Is a 'Depopulation Plan Orchestrated by UN' Amid Disturbing Rise in Conspiracy Theories," October 31, 2020, https://www.independent.co.uk/news/world/americas/us-election-2020/us-polls-election-2020-trump-covid-lies-conspiracy-b1403876.html

Bronner, Gérarld. *La démocratie des crédules*. Paris: PUF, 2013.

Caron, Jean-François. "On Human Nature and How to Control It." In *The Prince 2.0 : Applying Machiavellian Strategy to Contemporary Political Life*, 23–32. London : Palgrave MacMillan, 2019.

———. "The Western Model of Liberal Democracies and the Need for Authority." In *A Sketch of the World After the Covid-19 Crisis: Essays on Political Authority, The Future of Globalization and the Rise of China*, 5–21. London: Palgrave MacMillan, 2020.

Constant, Benjamin. "The Liberty of the Ancients Compared with that of the Moderns." In *Political Writings*. Cambridge: Cambridge University Press, 1988.

Crocker, Jennifer, Riia Luhtanen, Stephanie Broadnax, and Bruce Evan Blaine. "Belief in U.S. Government Conspiracy Theories Against Black Among Black and White College Students: Powerlessness or System Blame?" *Personality and Social Psychology Bulletin* 25, no. 8 (1999): 941–53.

Graeupner, Damaris and Alin Coman. "The Dark Side of Meaning-Making: How Social Exclusion Leads to Superstitious Thinking." *Journal of Experimental Social Psychology* 69 (2017): 218–22.

Grzesiak-Feldman, Monika. "The Effect of High-Anxiety Situations on Conspiracy Thinking." *Current Psychology* 32 (2013): 100–18.

Imhoff, Roland and Martin Bruder. "Speaking (Un-)Truth to Power: Conspiracy Mentality as A Generalised Political Attitude." *European Journal of Personality* 28, no. 1 (2014): 25–43.

Kant, Immanuel. *What is Enlightenment?* 1784.

———. *Critique of Pure Reason*. Cambridge: Cambridge University Press, 1998.

Leman, Patrick J. and Marco Cinnirella. "Beliefs in Conspiracy Theories and the Need for Cognitive Closure." *Frontiers in Psychology* 4, Article 378 (June 2013): 1–10.

Lewandowsky, Stephan, Klaus Oberauer, and Gilles E. Gignac. "NASA Faked the Moon Landing—Therefore, (climate) Science Is a Hoax: An Anatomy of the Motivated Rejection of Science." *Psychological Science* 24, no. 5 (2013): 622–33.

Pew Research Center. "Nearly Three-in-Ten Americans Believe Covid-19 Was Made in a Lab," April 8, 2020, https://www.pewresearch.org/fact-tank/2020/04/08/nearly-three-in-ten-americans-believe-covid-19-was-made-in-a-lab/?utm_source=Pew+Research+Center&utm_campaign=9a8a1fc2a0-EMAIL_CAMPAIGN_2020_04_09_06_59&utm_medium=email&utm_term=0_3e953b9b70-9a8a1fc2a0-400906701

Plato, *Phaedrus*.

Plato, *The Republic*.

Plato, *Gorgias*.

van Prooijen, Jan-Willem and Karen M. Douglas. "Belief in Conspiracy Theories: Basic Principles of an Emerging Research Domain." *European Journal of Social Psychology* 48 (2018): 897–908.

Roozenbeek, Jon, Claudia R. Schneider, Sarah Dryhurst, John Kerr, Alexandra L.J. Freeman, Gabriel Recchia, Anne Marthe van der Bles, and Sander van der Linden. "Susceptibility to Misinformation about COVID-19 around the World." *The Royal Society* 7, no. 10 (2020): 1–15.

Chapter Two

The Rights Revolution and the Evanescence of Authority

The phrase "you can't force me; I have the right to ..." has become a mantra that many of those living in liberal democracies have become accustomed to hearing. Indeed, many individuals have pushed the boundaries of their negative freedom to an extreme and have chosen to ignore the reasonable limits that ought to apply to them in a free and democratic society. During the COVID-19 pandemic, this mentality has led individuals to refuse to abide by justifiable rules and regulations meant to prevent the virus from spreading between individuals, such as the mandatory wearing of face masks in public spaces, limitations on the number of participants at gatherings and strict, mandatory quarantining upon returning from trips abroad. For instance, between May and September 2020, approximately 45,000 fines were given in France to individuals who refused to wear a mask while outside (Le Figaro 2020). After the establishment of a curfew in early 2021 and the banning of gatherings between individuals not belonging to the same "family bubble" in the province of Quebec, Canada, hundreds of fines were given to individuals who ignored these rules. In the midst of the first wave of the pandemic in the Spring of 2020, Italian authorities imposed fines on more than 110,000 people who had no legitimate reason for not respecting the lockdown or who lied on forms about their excursions (Duncan 2020). Meanwhile, in Germany, numerous protests have been organized on a regular basis since June 2020 by a movement called "Querdenker" (meaning "lateral thinker") whose members argue that the government policies have been threatening the right to freedom of opinion, expression and assembly guaranteed by the country's constitution. What can explain such irresponsible behaviour during a deadly pandemic? Why are individuals looking to bypass measures that are proportionate to the threat being faced? Answering this question is obviously a complex and multifaceted matter, and this is what this chapter will discuss.

First, we cannot ignore the fact that politicians may be, in part, responsible for the lack of respect for their authority. Indeed, it is curious how they can expect citizens to respect the work of members of the political elite and trust them when an almost endless number of them have been involved in dubious or criminal affairs, thus giving the impression that they sometimes break the law or instrumentalize their positions to serve their private interests. This "do as I say, not as I do" mentality therefore tends to generate suspicion over the "true reasons" behind politicians' decisions. In such circumstances, it is hardly unexpected that an increasing number of individuals are voicing their distrust of politicians and questioning their decisions. The lack of dedication to the common good such politicians have previously shown simply adds to the institutionalized distrust upon which the dynamic between the people and their leaders is established in liberal democracies, as the actions of the latter have simply proved the theory of the former right. The situation has reached a point where only 17% of Americans believe that their government is doing the right thing either "just about always" (3%) or "most of the time" (14%) (Pew Research Center 2019). This tends to perpetuate a vicious circle. As the field of politics and those involved in it are being increasingly denigrated, less talented but dedicated individuals are now willing to spend their time and effort in this profession, leaving the door wide open for less scrupulous people who see politics not necessarily as a way to serve the greater good but rather to pursue their own self-interest. This further damages the main pillar of trust, namely, the belief that those in charge of enacting common rules are reliable, competent and honest. This dynamic then creates fertile ground for a "trust vacuum" that will favour the rise of populist and anti-establishment leaders who can successfully challenge traditional politicians by effectively manipulating citizens' appetite for greatly needed change. This has been part of the secret behind the recent accession to high office of unlikely individuals such as Donald Trump, Boris Johnson, Volodymyr Zelensky and Rodrigo Duterte, whose sometimes violent diatribes against traditional politicians has struck a chord with people.

However, such a trust vacuum may also be explained by a structural problem associated with what is now the purpose of politics, that is, the capacity of the state to guarantee its citizens' right to pursue happiness and its ability to make a positive difference in people's lives. Indeed, to a large extent, politics has become meaningless and is no longer the mechanism through which societies are able to freely self-govern. In contrast, over the last 50 years, societies have gradually lost their aptitude to exercise autonomy, particularly because they are unable to control the powerful forces of finance, global trade and international markets. In a way, globalization has deprived them of the revolution the Enlightenment promised people: the rejection of heteronomous forces that deprive individuals and societies of their right to determine their own conception of happiness. At the level of political communities, this revolution has involved the capacity of citizens to have a genuine impact on the determination of policies and, accordingly, their capacity to amend such policies as needed in the event that they produce negative side effects. This is, in fact, the true meaning of citizenship and the way in which being a citizen differs from being only a subject. Those who fall within this latter category are simple pawns who can be used and abused without any need to be consulted. This used to be the case before when the outside forces of religion and traditions as well as the will of absolute monarchs dictated people's lives. Unfortunately, this fundamental promise of modernity has been hindered by globalization, as the economic sphere has clearly managed to free itself from the control of the people through the political sphere. As a result, politicians no longer have control over the forces of the global economy. On the contrary, such forces are rather subjected to fluctuations over which politicians have no control. By losing control of the economic sphere, the political sphere has become unable to enact policies that instrumentalize the state economy as a tool of collective prosperity and happiness. Globalization has, on the contrary, sounded the death knell of the welfare state, which has been defined as a democratic way of ensuring greater equality and creating opportunities for the state to enact economic policies that will benefit the whole of society. States can no longer pursue that objective when everything is left to the mercy of the uncontrollable flows of labour and capital in the global market. Today, territoriality and sovereignty no longer have the meaning they had before the emergence of globalization. Indeed, how is it possible to plan anything other than austerity measures when companies can rapidly delocalize and outsource their production, thereby leaving behind hundreds, if not thousands, of jobless employees? What sort of control do states currently have over their currency when enough traders acting together can create a crisis in a matter of hours through speculation as was the case with the collapse of the British pound in 1991, the Scandinavian currencies in 1992–93 and the Mexican peso one year later? This economic reality has created the not-so-false impression that politics is now meaningless and parliaments are simple consultative bodies whose power over aspects that have an effect on people's lives is mainly theoretical. This leaves behind the sour taste of collective powerlessness and a sense of fatality regarding individuals' capacity to change things and implement policies that will serve their interests. In a way, Lincoln's famous quote about the U.S. having "a government of the people, by the people and for the people" rings rather false when uncontrollable forces dictate state policies, as is currently the case. With the evolution of globalization, politics has gradually lost its meaning as an important sphere and is increasingly perceived as a farce. Unsurprisingly, the feeling of disappointment in and mistrust of those who had presided over this loss of meaning has increased during the same period of time.[1]

1 While than 70% of US Americans trusted their government in 1958, this feeling has seen a steady decline ever since, with the only notable exceptions being when the United States was at war in 1991 and in the weeks that followed the attacks of 9/11 (Pew Research Center 2019).

Consequently, it is not surprising to see that individuals whose core electoral promises were about giving back hope to people by regaining control over these heteronomous forces have been able to gain so much unexpected success despite their unconventional behaviours and public comments. In fact, the loss of control over people's destiny calls for a change of paradigm and a rejection of the usual conventions that traditional politicians—who are now seen as having failed miserably at their task of ensuring our happiness and freedom—have helped us become accustomed to. Disenfranchised people who have lost faith in the current order and who do not see any hope of seeing real change in their lives now want a new approach to a new world, which is why unconventional politicians who are very often the sources of conspiracy theories are beloved by a significant number of individuals: they represent the promise of a better and more controllable world, and their message therefore clashes violently with those representing the conventional establishment. This is what "Trumpism" is all about: it is a neologism defined around the desire of people to contest power by gaining power themselves in order to steal from the powerful, in the manner of Prometheus, what ought to belong to the people.

The COVID-19 crisis has illustrated that politics lack control over the economy, and this has provided ammunition for those who had already lost faith in those ruling their societies. A clear example is certainly when individuals realized that the production of strategic goods had been outsourced by companies, leading to a lack of medical and protective equipment, such as medical masks and ventilators, and that a significant percentage of the material necessary for active medicine components is produced in Asia, which has become the "factory of the world."[2] In this sense, globalization has revealed states' vulnerability in their obligation to protect the lives of their people. The overall assessment of politics now held by a growing number of people is therefore that politics combines incompetence and an inability among those in positions of authority to protect people's natural rights. This vision is fuelled by the impression that politicians have relinquished

---

2   China's share of global manufacturing value represented 28% in 2018, while it was only 1% in 1990.

their responsibilities to heteronomous forces over which they have lost control and by the documented dishonesty of the many politicians who have transformed the view of politics from being a noble activity dedicated serving the common happiness of all citizens to being an opportunity to enrich oneself at the expense of society. Consequently, when politics fails in such a way, it is not surprising if many individuals have simply lost faith in those who in power and no longer see the need to trust them or abide by their rules.

While the crisis of political authority can be explained in part by these conjectural elements, it also has roots in the "rights revolution," which has pushed the idea as the dominant doxa in liberal societies that all people have equal rights to be free and to pursue their own conception of what constitutes a good life, thereby overshadowing any form of dedication to anything higher than oneself. As I have already written elsewhere, this revolution has been the realization of Max Stirner's dream described in his book *The Ego and His Own*, in which he famously criticized the failure of the Enlightenment to provide people with the pure and absolute freedom of only serving themselves (Caron 2020, 5–21). In contrast, as I argued in the previous chapter, the abdication of one's will to the forces of religion has simply been replaced by secular forms of religion such as nationalism and ideology. However, starting in the 1960s, a second modern revolution occurred that had more radical aims than the one that took place in the 18th century and has gone unnoticed because of its peaceful nature in contrast to the latter. With their radical modernity, liberal societies have embarked on a revolutionary pattern that has led to the absolute sacralization of individual rights in such a way that the connection between individualities and the community has been eliminated. This shift has been described by Samuel Walker in the following way:

> This revolution includes a broad array of formal rights codified in laws and court decisions; but even more important, it involves a new rights consciousness, a way of thinking about ourselves and our society. As some observers point out, this new "rights culture" is marked by an almost reflexive habit of defining all problems in terms of rights. The words, expressed as demands, fall quickly from our lips: "I have a right to ..." These rights include an expectation of personal liberty, freedom from unwarranted government regulation

of both public and private matters, a right to speak freely on public affairs, and a freedom to conduct our private—including especially our sexual— lives as we choose. (Walker 1998, vii)

By codifying the supremacy of individual rights in law and court decisions, liberal societies have relegated themselves to respecting subordinate-level values that are now seen as preventing them from being authentic to themselves. This logic has had marked effects on the mentality of people who have come to place higher import on values such as self-expression and self-realization in a way that makes dedication to a higher cause look odd to many of us. Moreover, as I will explain in the next chapter, some groups have also been granted rights as a way to prevent discriminatory societal rules that might hinder their members' capacity to enjoy the right to fully benefit from their individual freedom, including, for example, enjoying freedom of religion. In both cases, critics argue that this logic has led to the erosion of a common sense of community and to the ghettoization of ethnocultural groups who now have the capacity to reproduce their values outside of their homeland and who no longer feel the need to integrate themselves within the broader society to which they only belong from a formal perspective.[3] When this is the case, sub-societal forms of authority or specific cultural beliefs that have been encouraged to exist as a constitutive condition for the sake of not harming their believers' individual freedom tend to clash with the broader authority of the state and will encourage disobedience to state laws or decrees.

Of course, and in accordance with traditional liberalism, individual rights are not absolute. In contrast, restrictions to their enjoyment can be imposed when the interest of the general public requires it. When this is the case, the limitations must be rationally connected with the objective being pursued by the state and should not impair the exercising of such rights any more than is required to accomplish that objective. However,

3   More precisely, by having acquired citizenship in the country to which they or their parents have immigrated, they are legally members of that society and can accordingly enjoy its political and legal rights. However, enjoying these formal rights does not necessarily mean that they are psychologically attached to the society that grants them these legal guarantees. This is why there is a need to distinguish between formal citizenship and a felt sense of attachment to a community.

liberal societies have witnessed a growing asymmetry between that philosophical logic entrenched in court jurisprudence[4] and political culture. Indeed, if these two dimensions were operating in synergistically, we would expect individuals to restrict on their own some of their actions when the common good requires it. Unfortunately, this is not what the COVID-19 crisis has revealed. In contrast, individuals have displayed behaviours and actions that are manifestly deleterious to their society's efforts to flatten the curve of infection at all stages of the pandemic: an attitude that clearly demonstrates how the sense of community and the normal constraints that ought to be associated with common life are now deemed obstacles to personal autonomy and freedom. For instance, at the peak of the health crisis in the Spring of 2020, many Italians refused to obey the government's directive to abide by the law and stay at home. People felt that their negative freedom was more important than what was in the public interest, so the usual lines and crowds of people were still evident in Italian *caffès* and restaurants, and some people openly bragged about how they were able to have drinks with friends in establishments outside of the locked-down zones by taking rural roads to elude police checkpoints (Horowitz and Bubola 2020). In Canada, reports emerged of people who had tested positive for the virus refusing to obey the quarantine they were required to follow, while polls in countries deeply affected by the virus have shown the reluctance of numerous people to follow the recommendations of their public authorities. As an example, in March 2020, a Belgian poll showed that nearly 50% of people aged between 18 and 21 were not respecting the confinement measures (overall, that number was 23% of the population). Even worse, the survey showed that only 24% of people who had experienced one symptom of the virus and 39% of those who had experienced at least two symptoms were respecting strict measures of confinement (RTBF 2020). In France, the imposition of strict confinement measures in mid-March 2020 did not prevent people from defying them: ten days after their implementation, more than 225,000 people had already been fined for not respecting the

---

4 We can consider in this regard the "Oakes Test" in Canada (R. *v.* Oakes, [1986] 1 S.C.R. 103).

measures (Sud-Ouest 2020). Finally, in December 2020, it was reported that thousands of Canadians—some of whom were members of provinces' legislative assemblies—had chosen to ignore the government's urge to refrain from going on vacations abroad at a time when more contagious mutations of the virus had appeared in Great Britain, Brazil and South Africa and when it was still unknown whether the vaccines that were starting to be administered were effective against those mutations. Reports also showed that many of these travellers did not respect their mandatory 14-day quarantine upon their return. These are just a few examples of irresponsible forms of citizenship that were triggered by the belief of many that their right to do what they wished could not be hindered by any other considerations, even those that ought to be respected by any rational individual during a pandemic.

These examples clearly show the disconnect between the judicial/philosophical logic of liberalism and the way the exercising of individual freedom is understood by many of us, as a significant number of citizens do not believe that limitations on their liberty are illegitimate. As a result, this mentality has slowly led to the erosion of the common anchoring of societies by undermining the values, ideas, and sources of pride that once united people. Having emphasized people's right to authenticity, it has encouraged them to emancipate themselves from all forms of power that are currently perceived as heteronomous forces contrary to their autonomy. Consequently, dedication to religious beliefs or the nation has become a form of renunciation of oneself. Similar to the way the main character in Albert Camus's *L'Étranger* (Meursault) is perceived by the other members of the community for not abiding by the usual norms, those who evoke the idea that people have a duty of loyalty to their community are now seen as *strangers* in a world in which these values are treated with suspicion as a potential threat to our freedom or even no longer matter. With time, the results of this deliquescence become not only political but also moral, as people begin to think that their inherent right to do what they want is best expressed in an unrepentant manner. This happens when people openly brag about how they have managed to escape a curfew or a city lockdown to enjoy a drink with their friends during a deadly pandemic. Even the natural ties of family have been a victim of this downward spiral due to the overemphasis liberal societies have placed on the supremacy of individual rights over any other social considerations. This is evidenced by the fate of the 15,000 elderly French citizens who in 2003, having been left alone by their children who preferred to enjoy their Summer holidays at the beach, died alone in a terrible heatwave. This latter example also reveals another pattern that has derived almost naturally from the second modern revolution, namely, that individuals have come to treat all their obligations towards others—even natural ones—simply as exchanges that last only as long as it benefits them. Once those obligations lose this value, individuals feel no qualms about dropping them. In other words, we tend to believe in the value of community only insofar as the presence of others is valuable to us.

This cultural crisis, of which respect for political authority is a prime victim, creates a paradoxical situation that can ultimately endanger the enjoyment of individual rights. Indeed, when individualistic behaviours pose a potential threat to other people's health during a pandemic, it is obvious that such behaviours are being denounced by people who rightfully see them as unacceptable and dangerous. This situation has also led to growing calls to implement harsher measures akin to those of a police state or authoritarian regime. Calls for lockdowns, curfews and police forces patrolling the streets at night to fine irresponsible citizens are perfectly understandable from the perspective of those who wish to remain safe, but it is also symptomatic of the excesses of individualism. Paradoxically, the unrestricted enjoyment of negative freedom on the part of many people will inevitably create the need for strict measures that imply force and violence—notions that are, in themselves, a natural reaction when authority has failed, which can be interpreted as the first move towards authoritarianism. Paradoxically, instead of allowing us to become free and enlightened citizens able to determine by ourselves what responsible actions we ought to take, the erosion of everything once perceived as more valuable than individuals' freedom—including political authority—has, on the contrary, led to our infantilization and the growth of political power over the populace. This trend increases in times of crisis, as was skilfully argued by Bertrand de Jouvenel in 1945. When people's lives are at stake, the terrifying feeling of being alone and not having any bonds with a community may lead individuals to become blind subjects to authority once again, waiting and expecting to be led by an omnipotent state. This fate is the natural outcome of people enjoying their freedom in an irresponsible fashion. When the community collapses and people are left alone in the face of a deadly virus, only one option becomes available: the imposition of strict measures by a Leviathanesque power that everyone will welcome with open arms.

This is where the Western model may be seriously threatened. Benjamin Constant and Alexis de Tocqueville have already warned us about the danger of tyranny emerging out of the over-enjoyment of negative freedom, and the erosion of authority caused, in part, by this same phenomenon may lead to similar consequences. In the long run, the goal is not to entirely sacrifice the core principles of liberalism but to contain them to avoid the current state of their excess. What ought to be avoided is an excessive response to the rogue individualistic behaviours we have seen emerge from this crisis, as this may lead to the implementation of policies that will bring long-lasting structural changes to liberal societies—policies that have proved to be dangerous slippery slopes in other similar circumstances. Unfortunately, the swing of the pendulum is uneven in this regard, and many liberticidal measures—similar to those imposed in authoritarian regimes—that are anti-nomic to what they stand for have been either implemented or suggested. This is by far the greatest collective defeat of liberal democracies that this crisis has highlighted. For instance, when the virus first hit the United Kingdom, the public itself asked the government to shut down public life and impose liberticidal measures (Hellyat 2020). Likewise, in France, many citizens said that they would have been willing to see the government impose harsher measures than those that were implemented in March 2020, including resorting to the military to regulate people's movements. The same sentiment was seen in Switzerland, where several people felt that even the strict confinement measures imposed by the federal state were insufficient (RTS Info 2020). However, the most extreme of these cases has probably been in Hungary, where the parliament granted Prime Minister Viktor Orban the right to rule by decree for an unlimited period of time. Those who opposed this measure were accused of hampering efforts that had to be made to fight the virus and of showing utter disrespect for the lives of Hungarians. It is difficult to combat this kind of rhetoric when people are genuinely afraid of contracting a deadly virus.[5] However, the impression has been growing in Western states that the initial measures ordered by liberal states did not lead to the same effective outcomes as those that were implemented in authoritarian countries (Kleinfeld 2020). Thus, the model adopted by the latter has largely been perceived as the one that ought to have been followed. Whether or not this is actually true, the fact remains that many people believe it is true. Therefore, there have been many opportunities for the abuse of power. When people are in desperate need of authority, as is the case with this pandemic, resistance is often scant. Once people have been told that these measures have been shown to be effective in fighting this virus, they may also think of them as being impactful in preventing or fighting other social problems. There are indeed serious reasons to fear that these liberticidal measures will outlast the virus, as Edward Snowden noted when he said, "When we see emergency measures passed, particularly today, they tend to be sticky" (Macaulay 2020), and by Douglas Rutzen, who argued that while "It's really easy to construct emergency powers, it's really difficult to deconstruct them" (Gebrekidan 2020). The Patriot Act is a good example of this phenomenon. While it was initially designed as short-term legislation that intended to help government agencies combat terrorism, this law has been regularly renewed and has now become a common tool used by the US government for cases that have nothing to do with antiterrorist purposes.

In this regard, people's privacy is at stake due to the measures that were first enacted by authoritarian regimes to use Internet data to better track the virus and were then considered by liberal democracies. For example, the Singaporean government used Bluetooth signals from cell phones to determine whom infected persons had been in contact with and for how long. In China, citizens were required to report details about their movements in public places and were contacted and requested to quarantine if it was found that they had been

---

5   As was said by a foreign businessman in China, "I do not really care about my freedom as long as I remain safe" (Vailles 2020).

in the vicinity of an infected person. Using personal data for such reasons may be valuable and justifiable, but if these data are not encrypted, third parties may also obtain access to them. There is no guarantee that such methods of determining individuals' whereabouts will stop being used once this health crisis is behind us. If these methods remain active, state agencies may be tempted to use them in combatting different social problems that are not related to public health.

There is another impact that the "rights revolution" has had on respect for authority that deserves to be mentioned, namely, the belief that people's inherent equality delegitimizes hierarchies. Indeed, the predominance of this notion has led to the re-establishment of organizations on new foundations, namely, the fear of leadership, as recognizing leadership is seen as an unwelcome form of anti-equalitarian submission to the will of individuals who will undoubtedly end up abusing their power to serve their own goals. This has been the case with many organizations whose ideology is directly derived from the "rights revolution"—mostly left-wing groups—who no longer have leaders but rather use "spokespersons" and whose internal management is no longer hierarchical but "collegial," in the style of what has been described akin to "politburos." As I have said previously, this phenomenon is reinforced by the various technologies now at people's disposal that allow them to access information that gives them the impression of expertise. The recent case of the "yellow vest" movement is a good example in this regard, as it is at the same time a denial of political authority and a refusal to organize around a hierarchical model that would naturally lead to a handful of individuals having power over the rest.

Angered by the fact that they no longer have a say in a system rigged by elites who cannot be trusted, either because they have given up any genuine influence to outside forces or because their time in office is simply a way for them to enrich themselves, the "yellow vest" movement was the quintessential incarnation of what I have described so far, namely, a world where the elite and the people clash violently. Even if the initial impetus behind its mobilization was the desire to cancel a tax imposed by the French government, the movement quickly turned into opposition against the political elite: opposition fuelled by the Promethean politicians who acted as a fifth column within the system itself. In fact, their main revendication became that the government—which had been elected only a few months before—resign. However, from an organizational perspective, what was striking about the movement was its lack of leadership, which made it virtually impossible for the government to find interlocutors with whom they could discuss matters. In contrast, whenever someone rose up as a potential leader, that person was immediately denounced or criticized as an authority and was seen either as anti-equalitarian or as bearing something similar to the mark of Cain seen upon politicians, who are untrustworthy, incompetent and selfish agents. When societies have reached a point where authority is perceived in such a way, authority becomes seen as a rotten tree that needs to be cut down.

Conclusion

The "rights revolution," which has informed a second and more radical modern revolution, has achieved the philosophical aspirations of the Enlightenment by liberating humans from the chains that prevented them from truly following their own conception of what constitutes a good life. It has liberated individuals from all limitations and has led to a profound crisis of authority, which has come full circle during the COVID-19 pandemic. For the reasons evoked in this chapter, politics is now perceived by many as a farce—and for good reasons in my opinion—and it is no wonder that the authority of those in charge has no influence over people who now act independently of what is objectively and rationally the right thing to do and will rather favour what is good for them. Furthermore, as I have quickly stated in this chapter, this second modern revolution has also had an impact on the valorization of sub-national religious and cultural beliefs—a phenomenon with roots in the inherent logic that has driven the "rights revolution" and has the potential to further erode the authority of the state. As I will explain in the next chapter, when these beliefs have a greater impact on people's actions than respect for the broader political authority of the state does, the impact on the general interest can be tremendously negative, especially when societies are facing a pandemic such as this.

References

Caron, Jean-François. "The Western Model of Liberal Democracies and the Need for Authority." In *A Sketch of the World After the Covid-19 Crisis: Essays on Political Authority, The Future of Globalization and the Rise of China*, 5–21. London: Palgrave MacMillan, 2020.

Duncan, Conrad. "Coronavirus: Italy charges nearly 110,000 people for breaking lockdown rules as tougher sanctions introduced," *The Independent*, March 26, 2020, https://www.independent.co.uk/news/world/europe/coronavirus-italy-lockdown-police-charges-fines-quarantine-lombardy-a9427046.html

Ellyat, Holly. "'Where Is Boris?': The UK Government Cautious Coronavirus Strategy Provokes a Public Backlash," *CNBC*, March 16, 2020, https://www.cnbc.com/2020/03/16/coronavirus-uk-public-backlash-against-lack-of-restrictions.html.

Gebrekidan, Selam. "For Autocrats, and Others, Coronavirus Is a Chance to Grab Even More Power," *New York Times*, March 30, 2020, https://www.nytimes.com/2020/03/30/world/europe/coronavirus-governments-power.html

Horowitz. Jason and Emma Bubola. "On Day 1 of Lockdown, Italian Officials Urge Citizens to Abide by Rules," *New York Times*, March 8, 2020, https://www.nytimes.com/2020/03/08/world/europe/italy-coronavirus-quarantine.html

Kleinfeld, Rachel. "Do Authoritarian or Democratic Countries Handle Pandemics Better?," Carnegie Endowment for International Peace, March 31, 2020, https://carnegieendowment.org/2020/03/31/do-authoritarian-or-democratic-countries-handle-pandemics-better-pub-81404

"Près de 45,000 verbalisations pour non-respect du port du masque depuis mai," *Le Figaro*, September 18, 2020. https://www.lefigaro.fr/flash-actu/pres-de-45-000-verbalisations-pour-non-respect-port-du-masque-depuis-mai-20200918

Macaulay, Thomas. "Snowden Warns : The Surveillance States We're Creating Now Will Outlast the Virus," *The Next Web*, March 25, 2020, https://thenextweb.com/neural/2020/03/25/snowden-warns-the-surveillance-states-were-creating-now-will-outlast-the-coronavirus/

"Public Trust in Government: 1968–2019," *Pew Research Center*, April 11, 2019. https://www.pewresearch.org/politics/2019/04/11/public-trust-in-government-1958-2019/

RTBF. "coronavirus: 44% des jeunes de 18 à 21 ans ne respecteraient pas les mesures de confinement," March 25, 2020, https://www.rtbf.be/info/societe/detail_coronavirus-le-confinement-une-tannee-chez-44-des-jeunes-de-18-a-21-ans-selon-test-achat?id=10467310

"Santé, quotidien, autorités, ce que pensent les Suisses du coronavirus," *RTS Info*, 25 March, 2020. https://www.rts.ch/info/suisse/11191960-sante-quotidien-autorites-ce-que-pensent-les-suisses-du-coronavirus.html

Sud-Ouest. "Coronavirus: plus de 225 000 verbalisations pour non-respect du confinement," https://www.sudouest.fr/2020/03/26/coronavirus-plus-de-225-000-verbalisations-pour-non-respect-du-confinement-7366241-10861.php

Vailles. Francis. "Un Québécois de Shandong dévoile la recette chinoise," *La Presse*, April 2, 2020, https://www.lapresse.ca/affaires/202004/02/01-5267709-un-quebecois-de-shandong-devoile-la-recette-chinoise.php

Walker. Samuel. *The Rights Revolution : Rights and Community in Modern America*. New York: Oxford University Press, 1998.

Chapter Three

When Cultural Beliefs Challenge Respect for Political Authority

After a lockdown of approximately 6 weeks imposed in the Spring of 2020, the citizens of the Republic of Kazakhstan in Central Asia were finally able to resume their normal life. Police roadblocks prohibiting entry into the country's capital, Nur-Sultan, and its southern metropolis, Almaty, as well as those restricting travel between the different districts within these cities, were lifted. Slowly but surely, after the middle of May, restaurants, shopping malls and bazaars were able to resume their activities but with severe restrictions, particularly in terms of the number of people allowed in these venues, along with the mandatory wearing of masks. While this area has regained its freedom, it has also remained subject to other prohibitions, the most important of which is the limitation on the number of people allowed at any form of gathering (marriages, funerals, or any other form of private get-togethers). However, after only a few weeks, the number of infected people began to skyrocket exponentially, so the government had no choice but to re-impose lockdown measures at the beginning of July 2020. Kazakhstan became the first country to impose a second lockdown.

This case, which hardly made international headlines, is, however, interesting and symptomatic of the lack of concern citizens have for demanding very clear rules on the part of the state despite the fact that this country is not considered as being a Liberal democracy.[1] Indeed, the rules of social distancing that remained in place and were strongly advocated for by both the Kazakhstani government and international organizations operating in the country—namely, the World Health Organization (WHO)—were ignored by many individuals, who continued to organize large family gatherings despite them being forbidden by the authorities. Such gatherings were publicly denounced not only by the head of the WHO Country Office, Caroline Clarinval,[2] but also by the Kazakhstani Deputy Prime Minister, Yeraly Tugzhanov, who was quoted as saying, "It is no secret that people have been secretly performing weddings, meeting with their families, and doing get-together events. Because of their thoughtless actions, people end up in hospital beds, to say nothing of the fatal cases. Each of us should be responsible not only for our own health but also for the health of our loved ones" (Satubaldina 2020b).

This situation shows the weight that customs and cultural traditions can have on people and how they can clash with political authority—even in authoritarian context—and go against the common good of the community. In this case, states' directives were offset by two cultural phenomena that combined to reinforce one another. On the one hand, it is important to maintain close ties with family members. Indeed, as noted by Zhanna Shayakhmetova, "social isolation and the phenomenon of 'living on your own' probably sound quite bizarre to most

---

1 Although Kazakhstan is not a Liberal democracy, it is nonetheless a good case-study for the purpose of this book. Indeed, Kazakhstan's authoritarianism is rather soft and allows its people to benefit from a large margin of freedom without experiencing the fear of being arrested, tortured or even worst. In this regard, people disregarding the sanitary directives imposed by the state did not have to face non-Liberal sanctions. In fact, the Kazakhstani authorities have rather imposed the same penalties against those disobeying, e.g. fines.
2 As she said, "At the same time, we are deeply concerned by the behaviour of the population. After easing the restrictions, not all people have been following the necessary precautionary measures, including maintaining social distance from, especially one's family" (Satubaldina 2020a).

Kazakhs" (Shayakhmetova 2016), and being hospitable to one's family members (even to unexpected visitors, who are referred to as a *kudaiy konak*, or "a guest sent by God") is a fundamental social tenet for them. This cultural feature is by no means surprising; many authors have previously described and explained the prevalence of family ties and obligations between members that are rooted in the earlier traditions of the nomadic Kazakh lifestyle from a time when the family unit (as well as the broader clan unit) was essential to their survival (Schatz 2000, 2004; Rigi 2004). These cultural norms, which include the ethical obligation to help one's family members, penetrates all levels of Kazakhstani society and has been identified as one of the principal reasons for the country's systemic corruption and nepotism, which Edward van Roy refers to as "the ethnocentric factor" (van Roy 1970). Unsurprisingly, the pervasiveness of this cultural feature has played a major role in the continued hosting of large family gatherings in Kazakhstan despite state directives forbidding them.

However, the importance of these gatherings cannot be fully appreciated without considering another important aspect of Central Asian culture, namely, the fear of experiencing *uyat* or "shame" due to refusing to attend these events. *Uyat* is a traditional custom in Central Asian republics and is used to regulate individuals' behaviours and encourage them to conform to dominant social norms.[3] Any deviation may lead the transgressor to be publicly shamed and stigmatized and ultimately to lose the social connections upon which a great deal depends (namely, finding a job) (Sataeva 2017, 25). When such a custom is prevalent, public shaming takes the form of what John Stuart Mill once referred to as social tyranny, which involves forcing people to change their preferred actions and instead abide by a certain set of rules and norms to avoid being judged and shamed in front of other people (Sataeva 2017, 25).

As a result, this tradition simply reinforced the importance of family gatherings, thus inhibiting compliance with the recommended practices of social distancing advocated by state authorities. Indeed, in

---

3 In line with what has been argued by anthropologist Collette Harris in her ethnographic research conducted in Tajikistan, the notion of shame (known there as 'aye') also plays a central role and exposes its victims to social exclusion (2004).

August 2020, a survey was conducted in four Kazakhstani cities with a total of 803 respondents (199 in Nur-Sultan, 204 in Almaty, 200 in Shymkent, and 200 in Petropavlovsk) in order to determine the prevalence of *uyat* and the impact it had on people's decision to flout the public directives by seeing their family members. Indeed, the survey revealed that 52.5% of the participants disobeyed the law by attending large family gatherings during the lockdown, and nine respondents who agreed to explain their reasons for disobeying the law confirmed that the fear of *uyat* played a major role in their decision to ignore the state's directives.

One respondent, who was invited to a wedding by her aunt's husband, said the following:

> It was super inconvenient for me to go there because I was not feeling well that day. However, I couldn't refuse even this kind of invitation from my aunt's husband because he is a very respected person in our family, and he does a lot for me. Finally, just because it was shameful (*uyat*) to say no, I went to this party.

Another participant from Shymkent shared the story of one of her relatives who had suffered from COVID-19 and left the hospital on the day of a wedding she had been invited to. Despite the fact that she was supposed to isolate for two more weeks, she went to the party anyway because she did not want other relatives to think that she did not respect them. This case demonstrates the power of *uyat*. The interviewee tried to explain such behaviour as follows: "It was shameful to skip the party of the oldest sister in the family, so she took a risk and chose to attend the wedding where there were about 40 people." Another participant shared a similar story. Again, a respondent's aunt was organizing the marriage of her son. The respondent had just checked out from the hospital and was recovering from COVID-19. The day of the wedding was just a week after she checked out. Initially, the sister-in-law refused to attend the wedding, but the groom's mother felt aggrieved by her decision. Realizing that their future relationship would suffer if she refused to go, she finally changed her mind and went.

Weddings are among the most necessary type of family gathering that one "must" attend when invited, as are funerals—respect should be paid to the person who has died as well as to his or her family. A man in Shymkent shared a story about the loss of his uncle during a period when cases of COVID-19 in Shymkent were growing rapidly. The interviewee and his brother tried to persuade their father, who had lost his elder brother to forego a traditional funeral. However, not only did their father refuse, but he stated that he "must go with tradition." Not only was it important for him to pay his respects to his brother, he also "had to" invite their friends and relatives to avoid *uyat*. The study participant and his brother persuaded their father to at least reduce the number of guests, and ultimately, "only" 80 people were invited.

This look into a country and culture unknown to many reveals something more fundamental about respect for public authority: cultural beliefs may take precedence over individuals' obligation to obey the law for the sake of the common good. In the Kazakhstani example, the survey revealed that the main source of shame emanates from closeminded family members and that individuals are generally not affected when they are shamed by public officials. As a result, public denunciations by government officials cannot counterbalance the embarrassment associated with not obeying the wishes and expectations of one's family members. In such a situation, when people have to choose between obeying the law and avoiding *uyat* from their family members, the latter option will prevail over the former. At the end of the day, responsible citizenship cannot prevail in such circumstances when cultural beliefs offset the legitimate objectives being pursued by the state for the sake of the common good.

Kazakhstan is, of course, only one example among many others. For instance, in Israel, many ultra-Orthodox Jews (who make up approximately 10–12% of the population) have refused to abide by the state's lockdown rules. As a result, the country has had one of the highest per capita rates of COVID-19-related death in the world, with the ultra-Orthodox community accounting for 40% of the country's infection cases (Rosenberg 2020). Similar to Kazakh culture, the largely collective way of life of ultra-Orthodox Jews makes them highly susceptible to being infected by the virus. Indeed, long hours spent together studying religious texts, daily prayers at the synagogue, and weddings and funerals, which can draw hundreds of people together, have transformed these gatherings into hotspots for the transmission of the disease. When confronted with the decision to abide by either their religious beliefs or the authority of the state, the members of this Jewish community have privileged the former over the latter. A similar sentiment was observed during the Spanish Flu pandemic, highlighting how beliefs have played an active role in the spread of the virus by encouraging people to behave in ways that are known to be hazardous for themselves and their loved ones. For instance, during the Spanish Flu pandemic, Canadian Catholics assembled in large numbers in churches to celebrate the three Christmas masses. A newspaper reported the following day that the crowds were so large that many believers could not even find a seat (Tanguay 2020). What prompted the gathering of these crowds was a mixture of people's sincere religious belief combined with a fear of being openly stigmatized by priests during their homilies. Indeed, at a time when religion played a pivotal role in people's lives,[4] any unwillingness to actively show their devotion and attend weekly religious services was noticed by priests, who did not hesitate to denounce the recalcitrant; this came with the risk of social ostracism—a fear accentuated by the fact that Quebec was, at the time, a rural region composed of small villages that disallowed our modern-day anonymity.

Needless to say, such situations present a great challenge for states, since the unwillingness to abide by government directives in favour of following what is dictated by one's cultural or religious beliefs rather than the state's authority has, for example, placed great pressure on national health care systems and has been detrimental to the sacrifices made by many to flatten the curve. In light of these examples, it is fairly easy to see that the possibility of the dictates of various beliefs or attachments clashing with broader respect for political authority has been a worry ever since the foundation of modern states. Indeed, states have always tried to favour a monistic sense of identity on the part of

---

4 This lasted until 1960 when a newly elected government implemented progressive policies and created a centralized system of public service that had the effect of radically diminishing the influence of religion. This period is known in Quebecois historiography as the period of the "Quiet Revolution."

their citizens, and they have thus chosen to directly or indirectly attack all forms of identity that might weak or clash with individuals' general identification with the state. During a pandemic, the necessity of having an overarching sense of attachment to the nation that takes precedence over parallel identities is fully evident when a sense of belonging to alternative communities endangers the lives of one's fellow citizens. This threat, as illustrated by Kazakh cultural norms and ultra-Orthodox Jewish religious beliefs, is therefore worrying, and unfortunately, we should not be surprised if these cases of parallel identities multiply over time in Western societies in a way that makes a state's political authority an impotent entity unable to impose its will on its citizens.

The reason we should be worried about this relates to the shift in liberal societies over the last several decades—a shift that is inherently connected with the previously discussed "rights revolution." Indeed, as has been argued previously, this logic was primarily aimed at increasing individuals' negative freedom by incorporating it into a constitution or charter of rights, but it has also led to the recognition and accommodation of minority groups. This aim has accelerated the decline of any form of dedication to a higher goal or entities other than oneself by developing a culture of "I have the right to," and the same outcome can also result from the strengthening of minority identities; this may come at the expense of the necessary broader sense of attachment that is required in every society, which may end up being weakened and subordinated to these specific sub-identities. In other words, the "rights revolution" has laid the foundation for a double attack on individuals' sense of civicism and, as a consequence, on their dedication to the common good. The glorification of the right to individuality and authenticity predominates, while the recognition of minority cultures has, for its part, the potential to create a new feudalism by making individuals more conscious of their differences and, as a consequence, transforming the common national sense of attachment upon which the will of the government lies into the sense of simply being one among many others.

I do not think that liberal societies have yet reached that point where minority cultures and beliefs are posing a significant challenge to broader senses of attachment on a massive scale. However, I believe that there are clear signs that these societies are about to move in that direction, primarily indicated by the attempts of minority groups to withdraw from common norms and by a growing tendency to erase from collective memory the myths and symbols that have historically been instrumental in the creation of a common imagined community. As a result, this shift has engendered a growing populist reaction from a significant segment of the population that is now actively denouncing such communities.

This situation begs the question of why there is a risk that minority beliefs will pose a direct threat to a broader sense of attachment in liberal societies. Through which intellectual acrobatics did the primacy of individual rights from the "rights revolution" turn into the consolidation of religious or cultural beliefs by granting minorities group-differentiated rights?[5] Indeed, this seems highly paradoxical, as these beliefs have always been seen as dogmas that have prevented people from exercising their own free will and from pursuing their own conception of what constitutes a good life. Justifying the recognition and accommodation of minority groups within liberalism has, on the contrary, always been an important component of liberal thinking, which considers the granting of group rights to primarily be a matter of individual rights and a way to complement the inherent shortcomings of the "rights revolution."

Indeed, by granting universal and equal individual rights, the "rights revolution" has given the false impression that the politics of equal dignity allows every individual an equal chance to fulfil his or her own conception of happiness. This is not the case, however, as social norms are not culturally neutral and may thus prevent individuals belonging to minority groups from enjoying the same rights as those who belong to the dominant ethnocultural group. For instance,

---

5 As Will Kymlicka writes, "To many people, the idea of group-differentiated rights seems to rest on a philosophy or world-view opposite to that of liberalism. It seems more concerned with the status of groups than with that of individuals. Moreover, it seems to treat individuals as the mere carriers of group identities and objectives, rather than as autonomous personalities capable of defining their own identity and goals in life. Group-differentiated rights, in short, seem to reflect a collectivist or communitarian out look, rather than the liberal belief in individual freedom and equality" (1995, 34).

the requirement to have specific, mandatory uniforms for the police or armed forces, include a photo on one's driving licence, and refrain from bringing weapons to school are all rules that have been considered discriminatory by members of religious or cultural minorities who have argued that such rules prevent them from enjoying their right to religious freedom. In attempting to prevent this situation from occurring, philosopher Charles Taylor has defended the necessity of implementing a "politics of difference" in liberal societies, which entails granting derogations from common rules (Taylor 1994). This differentiated treatment is considered to be a way for those affected by the discrimination caused by the false neutrality of public norms to have an equal right to religious freedom. In such cases, this treatment is not meant to offer special privileges to ethnocultural and religious minorities. It is rather a tool of equalization that makes the enjoyment of rights a practical reality rather than a symbolic fiction. This is why Sikhs are allowed to wear their ceremonial kirpan in some public places or to wear their turban instead of the traditional headwear dictated by their profession—whether that is a conventional police hat, military beret or wig worn by lawyers, barristers and judges in some countries.

Such differentiated treatment is not being granted only to ethnocultural or religious minorities. Indeed, is has also been given to individuals who, because of their socio-economic situation, also see the exercising of some of their fundamental rights being impaired. This is why court-appointed lawyers are often provided for free to individuals whose income falls below a certain level. Indeed, without such treatment, the right of individuals,—namely, poor individuals—to a fair and equal trial would remain entirely theoretical, as they would not otherwise have the resources to hire a competent lawyer to defend their cause, unlike individuals who have greater financial assets. Since economic disparities between individuals can cause discrimination and the incapacity of some to enjoy equal rights, such differentiated treatment is necessary and should be seen solely as a tool for equalizing rights. A genuine understanding of liberalism will therefore require accepting these exceptions.

Second, having a common culture has always been instrumental for the state to achieve its essential functions. Indeed, sharing a language and history generates a strong bond between millions of unknown individuals, and this sense of a common identity and common membership generates among such individuals the willingness to make sacrifices for each other. This common culture also facilitates the integration of individuals through the same "shared vocabulary of tradition and convention" (Kymlicka 1995, 77). Historically, immigrants have been expected to assimilate into their new culture—a process that has been encouraged through various means, such as the high bureaucratization of all aspects of people's lives that has forced newcomers to abide by the official state language and public schooling, which facilitates the full integration of the children of immigrants. Deprived of such institutional tools, a culture is doomed to disappear. Because of the pervasiveness of the new culture they are surrounded by, immigrants often quickly realize that assimilating themselves into their new culture is a valuable way to avoid social ostracism and poverty for themselves and their children.

Today, that situation has changed. Liberalism assumes—correctly, I believe—that we cannot understand freedom without culture and that caring about the former means respecting and recognizing the latter. Indeed, the capacity to make choices and evaluate their value is seen through the lens of culture. Without that filter, individuals would not have the tools needed to value certain practices over others. Taking this perspective, philosopher Will Kymlicka states the following:

> Whether or not a course of action has any significance for us depends on whether, and how, our language renders vivid to us the point of that activity. And the way in which language renders vivid these activities is shaped by our history, our traditions and conventions. Understanding these cultural narratives is a precondition of making intelligent judgements about how to lead our lives. In this sense, our culture not only provides options, it also provides the spectacle through which we identify experiences as valuable. (1995, 83)

As a result of this belief, liberalism cannot be distinguished from the necessary respect for culture, and there is, accordingly, a need to not cut off immigrants from their cultural heritage. This is why the "rights revolution" has led to a valorization of minority cultures and the expression of this valorization through various means, namely, anti-racist policies, affirmative action programs and efforts to portray immigrants in a positive way in official documents—such as school textbooks. The previously discussed solutions of derogation from clothing regulations or public norms have also been implemented in this regard. The overall objective of these polyethnic rights was not to allow immigrant groups to re-create their own societal culture by granting them their own institutional tools but rather to symbolically recognize and accommodate their differences as a way to show that the host culture is hospitable and willing to adapt itself, which is why these forms of recognition and accommodation have largely been seen as fundamentally inclusive.[6]

There are indeed fears that granting minority groups with their own institutions would result in the weakening of their bonds with the larger political community to which they belong, as is usually the case with national minorities—such as the *Québécois* in Canada, the Catalans in Spain and the Scots in Great Britain—that have been granted a right to self-govern through federalism or with other types of power devolution. Through these mechanisms, minority groups are acquiring the required tools for nation-building—a process that inevitably leads to the strengthening of national minorities' identity and, consequently, to a weakening of the ties that bind people together. This watering down of a strong and cohesive national identity can lead to negative social consequences. Indeed, for many liberal nationalists, a shared identity is an essential tool that serves many fundamental political purposes. David Miller notes that a common identity allows the state to legitimize

---

[6] Kymlicka writes the following in this regard: "Most polyethnic demands are evidence that members of minority groups want to participate within the mainstream of society. Consider the case of Sikhs who wanted to join the Royal Canadian Mounted Police, but, because of their religious requirements to wear a turban, could not do so unless they were exempted from the usual requirements regarding ceremonial headgear. Or the case of Orthodox Jews who wanted to join the US military, but who needed an exemption from the usual regulations so they could wear their yarmulka. Such exemptions are opposed by many people, who view them as a sign of disrespect for one of our 'national symbols'. But the fact that these men wanted to be a part of the national police force or the national military is ample evidence of their desire to participate in and contribute to the larger community. The special right they were requesting could only be seen as promoting not discouraging their integration" (1995, 177).

its decisions (Miller 1995), as it allows people to integrate within the same economical space, according to Ernest Gellner (1983), and because it ensures that citizens share essential virtues for their collective life. Kymlicka writes in this regard:

> [T]he health and stability of a modern democracy depends, not only on the justice of its basic institutions, but also on the qualities and attitudes of its citizens: e.g. their sense of identity, and how they view potentially competing forms of national, regional, ethnic, or religious identities; their ability to tolerate and work together with others who are different from themselves; their desire to participate in the political process to promote the public good and hold political authorities accountable; their willingness to show self-restraint and exercise personal responsibility in their economic demands, and in personal choices which affect their health and the environment; and their sense of justice and commitment to a fair distribution of resources. (1995, 175)

Maintaining unity in such a context has therefore been a difficult challenge for most multinational states that have faced succession threats of various degrees of severity. To prevent succession, these states have had to figure out ways to generate a form of federal patriotism among individuals belonging to national minorities that complements their national sense of attachment.[7] The relevance of this solution can hardly be challenged because the analysis of electoral behaviours of national minorities has proven that the supporters of secessionist parties in the past were those who did not identify with the broader state into which they were integrated (Keating 1997), which is why separatist leaders often unsurprisingly emphasized the incongruity of people having more than one sense of attachment (Mendelsohn 2002).

After decades of exclusionist and assimilationist approaches to immigration policies that were primarily aimed at welcoming

---

7   This solution is in line with the thinking of scholars such as Carl Friedrich, who wrote in 1968 that the survival of multinational states depends on the presence of a "federal spirit" (175) that is sufficiently strong to engender a sense of loyalty from all its citizens; Daniel Elazar, who argued that a federal state cannot survive without a form of political culture that relies on its citizens' willingness to work together (192–97); Samuel LaSelva, who speaks of federalism "as a way of life" (1996); and Jeremy Webber, who refers to the necessity of having a "federal conversation" (1994). See also Caron (2016).

individuals who were deemed compatible with the mainstream culture, most Western countries turned away from such policies and started to open their borders to groups that were previously seen as less able to assimilate into the dominant cultural creed. In the post-war period of the "Glorious Thirty," this decision was prompted by the need for unskilled manual workers. In other cases, the demise of colonial empires led countries such as France, Great Britain and the Netherlands to open their doors to former colonials, while Scandinavian countries offered generous asylum policies to individuals who were victims of persecution in non-Western societies (Alexander 2013, 540). At first, especially from the 1970s until the 1990s, these polyethnic rights were widely and actively supported by political elites who saw great benefits and advantages in cultural diversity (Brubaker 2001, 535). In this regard, the Canadian experience has been hailed as a success story (Caron 2012, Banting and Kymlicka 2010). However, this was rather an exception rather than the rule. Indeed, although it was not the intention behind that policy at the beginning, ethnic groups have since been able to find ways to acquire and develop mechanisms that allow them to re-create their old societal culture in their new home. This situation resulted not from the formal granting of autonomy to these groups, as is usually the case with national minorities but rather in informal manner; the result is nonetheless the same: the recognition of their beliefs has led to the consolidation of a societal culture that has enabled them to effectively maintain parallel feelings of attachment to the broader society by affirming their different cultural and political values. For the abovementioned reasons, this identity feudalism not only is related to the incapacity to generate a common sense of identification among millions of people (with its aforementioned consequences for solidarity and on other essential state functions) but is also a threat to the authority of the state, which can no longer prevail over these parallel identities that generate their own distinctive sets of rules and obligations. This ends up hampering the state's cohesiveness and its capacity to successfully implement collective goals, as the necessary broad civil solidarity becomes subordinated to the importance of primordial solidarities that tie loyalty to restrictive groups of individuals.

From a spatial perspective, these parallel communities have led to the residential ghettoization of minorities, which has allowed them to control small parts of a territory in which they have established their own formal institutions—such as schools—and have created networks that replace the state as the guarantor of intersubjective solidarity and socialization. As a result, these spaces are no longer under the control of the state (Rougier 2020). When this situation arises, these "states within the state"[8] and their inhabitants become self-sufficient, which prevents their integration into the larger state. There are some well-known cases of this, the most infamous being Molenbeek in Belgium and the Chapelle-Pajol district in northern Paris, where women are forbidden from going to local shops or restaurants and are regularly victims of verbal aggression when they "are not dressed properly." This phenomenon is happening elsewhere, and multicultural states are, to use the words of Trevor Philipps, "sleepwalking their way to segregation," as communities are slowly but surely becoming strangers to each other. The result is already known:

> these marooned communities will steadily drift away from the rest of us, evolving their own lifestyles, playing by their own rules and increasingly regarding the codes of behavior, loyalty and respect that the rest of us take for granted as outdated behavior that no longer applies to them. We know what follows then: crime, no-go areas and chronic cultural conflict. (Philipps 2005)

From Philipps's perspective, this process has the potential to create a vicious circle through which leading members of the ethnocultural majority segregate themselves from minority groups. Indeed, if the latter no longer consider themselves to be part of the collective we (sometimes to the point of wanting to replace the current societal culture with theirs, as was the case in Belgium, where an Islamic party named ISLAM was created to push for the imposition of sharia law around the country; to the point of attacking individuals who criticize their beliefs or ways of life, as in the case of the murder of Dutch filmmaker

---

8   In 1998, in light of the growing numbers of ethnic ghettos, Berlin Senator Jörg Schönbohm suggested that "Today there are neighborhoods where one has to say: this is not Germany anymore" (quted in Mennel, 139).

Theo Van Gogh in 2004; or to the point of waging war against the state, as was the case with those responsible for the 2004 and 2005 terrorist attacks in Madrid and London), the former may be tempted to instigate backlash against the politics of multiculturalism because they feel that their collective values are being threatened by immigrants whose beliefs are incompatible with their own and who simply do not want to become part of that "we." This backlash may also be fuelled by the growing distance emerging between groups and a decrease in intercultural contact. Lower awareness of the values, habits, customs and demands of minority groups who currently live in seclusion from other groups carries the possibility that such groups will become invisible to the majority, who may implement policies without taking into account the repercussions for the minority, thereby further increasing their sense of alienation.

This is because the emphasis on the legitimate need to tolerate, recognize and accommodate the beliefs and culture of minority groups has not been counter-balanced by the equally necessary integration of such groups within a unified cultural spectrum. In fact, because the myths, history and customs of the dominant ethnocultural group have been seen as either discriminatory or unconducive to integration, they have been gradually set aside, forming a slippery slope towards the abandonment of nationalism, that is, the celebration of a specific historical culture, in favour of a post-national form of nationhood defined by the absence of a core identity, as Canadian Prime Minister Justin Trudeau famously said in 2015 (Foran 2017).[9] Although the formerly popular melting pot model—or *creuset*—can be criticized for its illiberal nature, as it required immigrants and other minorities to abandon their original culture, it nonetheless led to their quick integration into a single national creed (Huntington 2004). When countries that opted for this model, such as the United States and France, were at war with states from which many of their immigrants originated, their efforts were not

---

9 It has to be noted that this hope of creating a post-national Europe was previously evoked in the 1990s by many authors and intellectuals in France, Great Britain, the Netherlands and in Germany. In this regard, see Vertovec (1996), Soysa (1994), Modood and Werbner (1997).

hampered by a fifth column that showed sympathy for foreign nations. In contrast, individuals of German or Italian descent did not hesitate to prove their loyalty to their new nation by either joining the military[10] or actively working in the war industry. In contrast, countries opting for the opposing path run the risk of meeting their moral obligations to individuals' freedom at the expense of national unity. As long as materialistic forms of integration, such as the ability to quickly integrate into a country's labour market and enjoy high standards of living levels of safety, exist, a country that has chosen the path of diversity can probably live without a common identity (Caron 2013). However, this is a very fragile foundation for unity, since when these forms of integration are lacking or failing, as is the case in many places in Europe where immigrants remain at the margins of the labour market, the chances are high that the call for patriotism will be ignored in favour of individualistic or culturally oriented behaviours when the country calls on its people to make sacrifices. Indeed, why would they be expected to defend an entity that has no meaning for them? To paraphrase Canadian novelist Yann Martel, a post-national state is very similar to a hotel: as long as its clients are able to enjoy warm meals, sleep in clean sheets and enjoy silence in the corridors and from adjacent rooms at night, they will most likely remain faithful customers. However, if these benefits begin to fade, they will take their loyalty elsewhere. In contrast, when they are not only customers but also stakeholders of the hotel who have an interest in seeing it succeed, the chances are higher that they will be inclined to make sacrifices and work together to solve the problems the hotel is facing.

This risk was highlighted at the beginning of the COVID-19 crisis in Europe and has clearly shown the limits of European identity, which are highly dependent on the economic advantages the EU provides its citizens.[11] Of course, this has led the most vocal anti-Europeanists, such as French polemist Eric Zemmour, who wrote that the crisis has revealed that the idea of a European people is simply a fantasy, to claim that they

---

10 For instance, the American 77th Division that was formed during WWI was so ethnically diverse that it was nicknamed "the Melting Pot Division."
11 The last part of this chapter is taken from Caron (2020), 23–39.

had always been right (Zemmour 2020). The pandemic has also forced European federalists, such as the French Minister of Finances, Bruno Le Maire, who clearly expressed his fear that the European Union would simply collapse if its member states maintained their selfish courses of action, to acknowledge the seriousness of the situation (20 Minutes 2020). The same fear was expressed by Paolo Gentilone, the European Union's economy commissioner: a refusal on the part of some states to show solidarity with those more affected by the virus would put their common project in jeopardy (Koutsokosta and Gill 2020). The most significant plea was, however, made by Jacques Delors, the former European Commission president who helped build the modern EU and who warned that a lack of solidarity between the European people constituted a deadly threat to the European Union (de Ravinel 2020). The cries of joy or fear regarding the possible collapse of this great political project are the result of various decisions and declarations made by EU officials that show how the European political community is an empty shell that sees solidarity simply as a rhetorical tool without any real implications. This is supported by Czech Republic's theft of masks that were destined for Italy in March 2020 as well as the debate over the "coronabond," the aim of which was to decrease the borrowing costs of some of Europe's most affected countries (namely, Italy and Spain) through the issuance of a common debt instrument, thereby preventing another economic crisis and providing these states additional resources to invest in their public health systems. After the plan was initially rejected by some states claiming that it would penalize states that had shown fiscal responsibility in the past and encourage those states that would have benefited from the plan to further mismanage their public finances, a more modest version was eventually adopted. However, the initial opposition, which was largely led by the Netherlands, simply condemned more so-called fellow citizens living in Italy and Spain to remain at the mercy of the virus.

This reaction perfectly illustrates the failure of the political project of the European Union. Indeed, a community or society needs to be more than just a union of random people who share nothing but a common passport and similar political rights. Citizenship must go beyond these mere judicial and political dimensions; otherwise, it is doomed to become a community of free riders who care about nothing but themselves. This health crisis has revealed the true state of the European Union, as nothing else has ever cemented the European peoples together long enough to produce a psychological sense of attachment that would generate a display of solidarity and a genuine willingness to make sacrifices for fellow citizens. Unfortunately, this sense of attachment cannot be derived purely from the materialistic advantages a society provides. Indeed, studies over the years have consistently shown that identification with the European Union is mainly instrumental and can largely be attributed to economic concerns. More precisely, there has been a strong correlation between those who have developed a European sense of attachment and those who have benefitted from the common market (Tucket et al. 2002), namely, educated and multilingual young professionals with transferable skills. Not only is it highly risky for a sense of identity to depend on such a notion, but such a tenuous base also unable to generate an ethical essence for a community. Indeed, since there will always be "winners" and "losers" in a liberal economy, the idea of linking economic benefits with attachment to a community is largely divisive, even though community spirit ought to be as inclusive as possible. Second, communities cannot be perceived as purely selfish instruments that allow people to further their own interests. This way of thinking creates a false feeling of attachment, as people may appear to be truly subjectively engaged with their work or community, but they are nonetheless profoundly detached from it. In reality, these people see their involvement and dedication solely as (in the case of employment) a means to gain valuable work experience or other personal benefits, such as obtaining a promotion or increasing their salary. At no point do they identify with these forms of attachment or develop any solidarity with their co-workers or co-citizens. Instead, whenever they are asked to make sacrifices for the well-being of these others, they are silent, as they feel that they belong only to themselves.

Communities must therefore be conceived of in a manner that bears some similarity to Aristotle's conception of politics: Aristotle believed that a genuine political community is inextricably linked with ethical considerations, the most important being justice and the capacity of its members to distribute the common wealth equitably among all.

This is why he discarded other forms of political association, such as military or economic alliances between city-states, as false communities, because of their purely instrumental nature.[12] Although Aristotle was by no means a liberal thinker in the sense that he thought that everything—even individual freedom—had to be subordinated to this quest for justice, he nonetheless reminds us of the necessary ethical essence of communities, the absence of which dooms them to erode and disappear at the slightest crisis. In contrast, when a community is organized around the belief that it is meant to realize a higher collective purpose, people will feel bonded to one another and will be willing to make sacrifices, the most important being solidarity with and regard for the well-being of the other members of the community. As stated before, people will come to see this feeling as a natural obligation and not as one option among many. In other words, solidarity is a natural common obligation, while charity is a voluntary action based on the presence or absence of good will and is generally shown towards those who are not part of a community. Based on this conceptual difference, it is rather easy to understand why nation-states—even liberal ones— dedicate a significant part of their national budgets to social programs, while the share dedicated to humanitarian aid—that is, to individuals living abroad—is an insignificant portion of the budget. In the former

---

12 Without referring to Aristotle, Emmanuel Macron has expressed that the absence of a community spirit in the European Union is the result of the fact that this supranational entity has never been more than a simple economic market. He said that The European nations have "decided to have a shared journey. If at this point in history we don't do it, there will no longer be any shared adventure. Because if we don't do this today, the populists will win. Today, tomorrow, the day after, in Italy, Spain and maybe even France and in other places. And in countries which are still against it today. It's obvious because they will say: 'What is this adventure you are offering us? These people will not protect us in times of crisis, they won't protect us the next day, they show us no solidarity. When migrants arrive, they ask us to keep them for ourselves. When an epidemic arrives, they ask us to handle it. They're great really. They are all for Europe when it's about exporting to our country the goods that they are producing. They are all for Europe when it's about having your labor and your markets and producing car parts that we no longer make in our own country. But they're not for Europe when it comes to mutualizing debt.' That's nonsense. But it's the reality. So we have reached that moment of truth when we must know whether or not the European Union is a political project or strictly a market plan" (Macron 2020).

case, social programs are perceived as obligations, while humanitarian aid is seen as an optional benefit. The coronavirus crisis has shown that the latter option has dominated the logic of EU leaders, who have refused to acknowledge their obligations towards their fellow citizens simply because they think of them not as fellow citizens but as strangers. In a nutshell, what we have seen at the European level may ultimately happen as well at the infra-national level where Liberal states have made the principle of recognizing and accommodating cultural or religious beliefs a pivotal idea of their constitutional and judicial architecture.

Conclusion

The COVID-19 crisis has given us a glimpse of what we can expect when different communities no longer abide by the authority of a state imposing decisions and directives for the common good but instead choose to follow what their specific cultural beliefs dictate. The multicultural paradigm associated with the liberalism of Western states runs the risk of turning what is still a marginal trend into a widespread phenomenon that could threaten the very existence of states. In this regard, we need to think beyond the current pandemic and consider what may happen when multicultural states face other crises in the future. What if a state is engaged in a war with another country whose culture bears more significance for citizens or residents of the former who immigrated from the latter? Would the former's war efforts be hampered by a lack of patriotism and even resistance on the part of these individuals? Already, we have seen numerous individuals leave their host country—or the country where their parents immigrated—and travel to Syria to fight alongside the Islamic State, which is a clear sign of a significant failure in integration.[13] The same worry surfaces in regard

---

13 In 2014, it was estimated that more than 3,000 Europeans had joined the ranks of the Islamic State in Syria and in Iraq. However, Gilles de Kerchove, the EU Counter-Terrorism Coordinator, estimated that there are approximately 50,000 jihadists living in Europe.

to violence that has been perpetrated by European citizens.[14] Moreover, in a segregated state, what sort of aid can we expect to see given from sub-groups that are not affected by a natural catastrophe to members of another group that have been so affected? These are worrying questions that require careful handling if we are to avoid extreme solutions. One thing that needs to be emphasized here is that immigration and diversity should not be seen as a problem, nor should the provenance of newcomers. What matters the most at the end of the day is states' capacity to find a balance between the tolerance and accommodation of the "other" and the necessary convergence of various peoples into a unified community, the dedication to which will ultimately supersede the importance of religious and cultural beliefs when the situation requires it. This is what the last chapter will discuss, along with providing a broader reflection on how liberalism is compatible with an ideal of "responsible citizenship" that requires people and groups to subordinate their personal happiness and cultural or religious beliefs to the greater good.

References

Alexander, Jeffrey C. "Struggling Over the Mode of Incorporation: Backlash Against Multiculturalism in Europe." *Ethnic and Racial Studies* 36, no. 3 (2013): 531–56.
Banting, Keith and Will Kymlicka. "Canadian Multiculturalism: Global Anxieties and Local Debates." *British Journal of Canadian Studies* 23, no. 1 (2010): 43–72.
Brubaker, Rogers. "The Return of Assimilation? Changing Perspectives on Immigration and Its Sequels in France, Germany, and the United States." *Ethnic and Racial Studies* 24, no. 4 (2001): 531–48.
Caron, Jean-François. "Rooted Cosmopolitanism in Canada and Quebec." *National Identities* 14, no. 2 (2012): 351–66.
———. "Understanding and Interpreting France's National Identity: The Meanings of Being French." *National Identities* 15, no. 3 (2013): 223–37.
———. *Être fédéraliste au Québec: Comprendre les raisons de l'attachement des Québécois au Canada*. Québec : Presses de l'Université Laval, 2016.

---

14 The list is long in this regard. We can include the 2015 Charlie Hebdo shooting by the Kouachi brothers, the Hypercacher kosher supermarket siege in January 2015 by Amedy Coulibaly and the November 2015 terrorist attacks by members of the Brussels ISIL terror cell that took place in various locations around Paris.

———. "The Resurgence of the Nation-State and the Future of Globalization." In *A Sketch of the World After the Covid-19 Crisis: Essays on Political Authority, The Future of Globalization and the Rise of China*, 23–39. London: Palgrave MacMillan, 2020.

de Ravinel, Sophie. "Le manque de solidarité est un «danger mortel» pour l'Europe, selon Jacques Delors," March 28, 2020. https://www.lefigaro.fr/politique/le-manque-de-solidarite-est-un-danger-mortel-pour-l-europe-selon-jacques-delors-20200328

Elazar, Daniel. *Exploring Federalism*. Tuscaloosa : University of Alabama Press, 1987.

Foran, Charles. "The Canada Experiment: It This the World's First 'Postnational' Country?" *The Guardian*, January 4, 2017. https://www.theguardian.com/world/2017/jan/04/the-canada-experiment-is-this-the-worlds-first-postnational-country.

Friedrich, Carl. *Trends of Federalism in Theory and Practice*, New York: Praeger, 1968.

Gellner, Ernest. *Nations and Nationalism*. Cornell : Cornell University Press, 1983.

Harris, Colette. *Control and Subversion: Gender Relations in Tajikistan*. London & Sterling: Pluto Press, 2004.

Huntington, Samuel P. *Who Are We? The Challenges to America's National Identity*. New York: Simon & Schuster, 2004.

Keating, Michael. *Les défis du nationalisme moderne : Québec, Catalogne, Écosse*. Montreal: Les Presses de l'Université de Montréal, 1997.

Koutsokosta, Efi and Joanna Gill. "EU Project in Danger If No Solidarity on Coronavirus Crisis, Says Economy Chief Gentiloni," *Euronews*, March 30, 2020. https://www.euronews.com/2020/03/30/eu-project-in-danger-if-no-solidarity-on-coronavirus-crisis-says-economy-chief-gentiloni

Kymlicka, Will. *Multicultural Citizenship: A Liberal Theory of Minority Rights*. Oxford: Oxford University Press, 1995.

LaSelva, Samuel. *The Moral Foundations of Canadian Federalism: Paradoxes, Alternatives, Achievements and Tragedies of Nationhood*. Montreal & Kingston: McGill-Queen's University Press, 1996.

Macron, Emmanuel. "Transcript: We Are at a Moment of Truth," *Financial Times*, April 14, 2020. https://www.ft.com/content/317b4f61-672e-4c4b-b816-71e0ff63cab2.

Mendelsohn, Matthew. "Measuring National Identity and Patterns of Attachment: Quebec and Nationalist Mobilization." *Nationalism & Ethnic Politics* 8, no. 3 (2002): 72–94.

Mennel, Barbara. "Bruce Lee in Kreuzberg und Scarface in Altona: Transnational auteurism and ghettocentrism in Thomas Arslan's *Brothers and Sisters* and Fatih Akins' *Short Sharp Shock*." *New German Critique*, 87 (2002): 133–56.

Miller, David. *On Nationality*. Oxford: Oxford University Press, 1995.

Modood, Tariq and Prina Werbner (eds.). *The Politics of Multiculturalism in the New Europe: Racism, Identity and Community*. London: Zed Books, 1997.

Philipps, Trevor. *After 7/7 : Sleepwalking to Segregation*, 2005, https://www.jiscmail.ac.uk/cgi-bin/webadmin?A3=ind0509&L=CRONEM&=quoted-printable&P=60513&B=%EF%BF%BD—_%3D_NextPart_001_01C5C28A.09501783&T=text%2Fhtml;%20charset=iso-8859-1&pending=

Rigi, Jakob. "Corruption in Post-Soviet Kazakhstan." In *Between Morality and the Law: Corruption, Anthropology and Comparative Society*, edited by Italo Pardo, 101–17. Farnham: Ashgate Pub Ltd., 2004.

Rosenberg, David E. "The Government Can't Save Ultra-Orthodox Jews From COVID-19. Religious Leaders Can," *Foreign Policy*, October 12, 2020, https://foreignpolicy.com/2020/10/12/the-government-cant-save-ultra-orthodox-jews-from-covid-19-religious-leaders-can/

Rougier, Bernard (ed.). *Territoires conquis de l'islamisme*, Paris: PUF, 2020.

Sataeva, Begimai. *Public Shaming and Resistance in the Context of Bride Kidnapping Phenomenon in Kyrgyzstan*. Utrecht: University of Utrecht, 2017.

Satubaldina, Assel. "People's Continued Negligence of Social Distancing Must Be Addressed, says WHO Director in Kazakhstan," *The Astana Times*, July 16, 2020a, https://astanatimes.com/2020/07/peoples-continued-negligence-of-social-distancing-must-be-addressed-says-who-director-in-kazakhstan/

———. "Kazakhstan to Reintroduce Two Week Lockdown to Deal With COVID-19 Spike," *The Astana Times*, July 3, 2020b, https://astanatimes.com/2020/07/kazakhstan-to-reintroduce-two-week-lockdown-to-deal-with-covid-19-spike/

Schatz, Edward. "The Politics of Multiple Identities : Lineage and Ethnicity in Kazakhstan." *Europe-Asia Studies*, 52, no. 3 (2000): 489–508.

———. *Modern Clan Politics: The Power of 'Blood' in Kazakhstan and Beyond*. Seattle: University of Washington Press, 2004.

Shayakhmetova, Zhanna. "Family Hospitality Traditions Keeps Kazakhstan Strong," *Astana Times*, November 1, 2016, https://astanatimes.com/2016/11/family-hospitality-tradition-keeps-kazakhstan-strong/

Soysa, Yasemin. *Limits of Citizenship: Migrants and Postnational Membership in Europa*. Chicago: University of Chicago Press, 1994.

Tanguay, Sébastien. "En 1918, la grippe espagnole tuait des millions de personnes ... mais pas Noël," Radio-Canada, December 25, 2020, https://ici.radio-canada.ca/nouvelle/1758931/noel-grippe-espagnole-1918-epidemie-quebec

Taylor, Charles. "The Politics of Recognition." In *Multiculturalism: Examining the Politics of Recognition*, edited by Amy Gutmann, 25–73. Princeton: Princeton University Press, 1994.

Tucker, Josh A., Alexander C. Pacek, and Adam J. Berensky. "Transitional Winners and Losers: Attitudes toward EU membership in Post-Communist Countries." *American Journal of Political Science* 46, no. 3 (2002): 557–71.

Van Roy, Edward. "On the Theory of Corruption," *Economic Development and Cultural Change* 19, no. 1 (1970): 86–110.

Vertovec, Steven. "Multiculturalism, Culturalism, and Public Incorporation." *Ethnic and Racial Studies* 19, no. 1 (1996): 49–69.

Webber, Jeremy. *Reimagining Canada : Language, Culture, Community, and the Canadian Constitution*. Montreal & Kingston: McGill-Queen's University Press, 1994.

Zemmour, Eric. "L'Union européenne, première victime du coronavirus," *Le Figaro*, March 20, 2020, https://www.lefigaro.fr/vox/monde/eric-zemmour-l-union-europeenne-premiere-victime-du-coronavirus-20200320

"Coronavirus: Bruno Le Maire estime que si l'UE n'aide pas l'Italie, elle ne s'en relèvera pas," 20 Minutes, March 20, 2020, https://www.20minutes.fr/economie/2744507-20200320-coronavirus-bruno-maire-estime-si-ue-aide-italie-relevera

Conclusion

In Defence of Responsible Citizenship

As I have argued so far, liberalism is an ideology that bears the fruits of disobedience. Indeed, the institutionalized mistrust towards those chosen to protect people's natural rights has undoubtedly played a role in this regard, as has the value given to individuals' rights to freely express their opinions and to be given equal importance to others, as well as the valorization of reason as the sole tool at our disposal for understanding the world around us. With the help of modern technology, all these elements have constituted a cocktail, which has made obedience to authority and respect towards authority figures a notion that has increasingly become foreign to many of us, while the cult of irresponsible self-indulgence has rather become the norm. Signs of this erosion were already visible throughout Western-type liberal democracies before the deadly coronavirus pandemic brought the world to a halt in the Spring of 2020. However, Covid-19 has provided an opportunity to witness on a broad scale—and with potentially tragic consequences—people's unwillingness to abide by perfectly simple sanitary rules. People have brazenly refused to wear masks in public or to refrain from participating in large gatherings, while others have openly opted to travel abroad at a time when more and more countries have faced an increase in the infectious mutations of the virus. This has forced states to implement harsh, liberticidal policies directly inspired by those of totalitarian China. In essence, the fact that states have resorted to these draconian measures must be interpreted as glaring evidence of people's lack of respect for political authority in liberal democracies. Demanded by citizens themselves, fed up with their co-citizens' irresponsible behaviour, a belief has emerged during this pandemic that only harsh restrictive measures ought to be considered, because placing trust in people to respect basic rules has proved futile. There is an inherent danger in a mindset that consists in resorting to such measures as the sole possible solution for a society facing such a crisis, whereby citizens are required to restrict their freedom. The risk is that such measures might become durable in the long term, thereby ultimately leading to a slow erosion of the rule of law and the preservation of freedom. Paradoxically, the demand for what is inaccurately seen as authority may ultimately lay the groundwork for an authoritarian and anti-liberal pattern.

There is, therefore, an intrinsic danger in seeing the State as the one and only way to protect one's individual freedom, to the extent that there is always an obvious risk of creating a momentum that might lead to excessive and disproportionate measures. This is, in my view, the wrong path to follow. The same logical conclusion ought to apply to those who advocate the revival of ancient forms of "ghosts" with which to establish values—whether religiously or culturally inspired—that would serve as a centripetal force from which a "collective we" could be generated. There is no doubt that creating ties, which would offset forces that tend to drive individuals and groups apart from one another, is a welcome proposal. The question, however, is how it might fit within a liberal framework. There are reasons to be sceptical about such nostalgia. In fact, and although this is a matter of perspective, I do not think that individuals would benefit from travelling back in time to eras in which religious dogmas were omnipresent, where individuals who stepped out of line were stigmatized, or when minorities had to submit to the rules and norms of a hegemonic culture. We have moved on from that age. The legitimate criticisms we ought to address against contemporary liberalism should not make us forget that the weight of community can be as liberticidal as laws and decrees, and that what appears to be an obvious solution can actually result in a less desirable situation. Subordinating the rights of people pursuing happiness for an enforced respect for a pre-defined conception of the good life which can only be restrictive is simply not an option for consideration. Out of this dialectic of extremes, between hyper-individualism and nostalgia for ancient times, must lead to the emergence of a balanced view, or a new synthesis, that will enable personal freedom to be enjoyed, but not at the expense of the community or of state authority during times of crisis.

We must go back to what liberalism originally stood for, which was the view that the State is not necessary for the guarantee of the protection of individuals' natural rights, and that people have an inherent capacity to act in a way that will not be detrimental to the capacity of their co-citizens to enjoy their freedom. I believe that individual freedom would gain from a situation in which the restriction of people's behaviour would not emanate from the State, but from individuals themselves, through a form of natural self-restriction based on practical public reason. In this regard, the political authority's main role should never be the imposition of laws and decrees that have the potential to go too far and, accordingly, deny people their freedom. On the contrary, it should rather be the symbol and the voice of the natural law of reason, in a way that will inspire people to embrace the same language despite their cultural or religious differences. Only this process can lead to a "responsible citizenship" that will remain within the bounds of liberalism and allow individuals to continue enjoying their personal freedom in a way that is reasonable in a free and democratic society.

In other words, this conception of citizenship requires the voluntary and conscious act of limiting one's own actions when one realizes they might negatively affect the lives or the rights of others. Since this limitation is not considered to be the result of effective constraints by the State, by means of its laws and other decrees, but rather purely out of Man's conscience, this idea to some extent resembles John Locke's earlier vision of a pre-political and natural respect between individuals. According to this theory, when a situation requires the limiting of one's freedom, individuals should feel the discomfort of an internal sense of guilt at the mere thought of ignoring the need to restrict their will. In an ideal world, conducive to the flourishing of freedom, this limitation of individual autonomy would depend, as was the case with Locke, solely on Man, thus rendering state intervention unnecessary and guaranteeing the *de facto* imposition of the most minimal restrictions on their freedom. Why indeed would Man impose exaggerated and disproportionate limitations on that which he holds dearest? For the absence of coercive laws imposed by the State is not synonymous with an ethical vacuum and an anarchical state where everything is subordinated to the licentiousness of the strongest.

Conversely, Locke was of the opinion that human beings are endowed with reason, dominated by a universal morality to govern intersubjective behaviour in a way that predates the existence of a formal state law which can unfortunately err and tyrannise individuals. Such individual reason, which of itself imposes limitations on human actions, is a natural consequence of the fact that individuals are not born to live in isolation from one another. This has been perfectly illustrated by the inability of our fellow citizens to live in isolation during the worst moments of the many quarantines imposed throughout the world, and which has led many to violate health rules. Consequently, the exercise of freedom can only be a social reality that has no choice other than to consider the interest of others, failing which humans would only be doomed to destroy each other: a behaviour which would then be unnatural insofar as the instinct for self-preservation is typical to all human beings. On a theoretical level, this is what the idea of responsible citizenship consists of, and why it constitutes the least detrimental solution to individual liberties, in that the restrictions individuals are called upon to impose on themselves emanate from themselves, not from a power superior to them and from which they cannot lose control.

Unfortunately, this natural restriction, operating as a natural law on individuals, was clearly lacking during the health crisis caused by Covid-19. The refusal by some people to adapt their behaviour, so as to minimize their impact on the lives and health of others, has shown a lack of civic-mindedness among some of us unable to simply consider the potential impact of their actions on others. In this case, there is reason to be sceptical about the capacity for human beings to project their freedom into its necessary collective dimension. Consequently, this seems to automatically bring us back to the potentially liberty-oppressive perspective that sees state-imposed coercive measures as the only way to ensure that everyone's rights and interests are respected. However, I do not think that this is a fate liberal societies are destined to experience. The lack of civicism we have witnessed in the course of this crisis is rather due to the overly individualistic extreme culture that has been the dominant cultural trend in liberal democracies ever since the end of the Second World War. This trend can be reversed by making practical public reason a fundamental cornerstone of liberal societies, rather than emphasizing people's right to enjoy their negative freedom.

As previously mentioned, submitting individuals' negative freedom to the imperatives of practical public reason is not a synonym of an illiberal policy. By contrast, it is rather how the degree of freedom individuals ought to enjoy can be assessed in such societies. Indeed, as I have already argued elsewhere (Caron 2014), this assessment is not open to relativism. On the contrary, despite their profound diversity and multiplicity of conceptions of the good life that we can find and that are encouraged to flourish in liberal societies, these communities can nonetheless be regulated around universal principles of justice. In order to achieve such a possibility, the consensus around the principles of justice should not lie on comprehensive or particular doctrines, but rather on universal norms that everyone can accept, despite their respective religious or cultural beliefs. Considering the deep pluralism of liberal societies, these universal norms, which can be discovered by any reasonable human being, are the only element people have in common that can allow them to organize their peaceful living together through a common vocabulary. This is where the Rawlsian notion of an "overlapping consensus" comes into play. This notion corresponds to the values that constitute the basic elements upon which every rational human being is able to accept. More precisely, this agreement will be possible through the use of public reason, which can be defined as the language of universal and transcultural principles of justice with which people can debate the finalities of their political community, in a way that does not refer to any particular religious doctrine. Since the principles inherent to an overlapping consensus are seen as inalienable and fundamental individual rights, everyone has the same capacity to question and assess their individual actions. Through its use, individuals are able to think rationally about the consequences of their actions and to accept that some of their behaviour is not acceptable because it will have negative implications on the lives of others. This was precisely the underlying premise of the regulations advocated by state representatives during the Covid-19 pandemic. Wearing a mask outside, avoiding unnecessary gatherings, postponing vacations on a Mexican or Cuban beach, are all reasonable limitations of one's personal freedom that can be understood by anyone, irrespective of their cultural or religious beliefs. Despite being present in all people's minds, this faculty of reason nonetheless remains a dormant feature of their psyche, since they have been accustomed to a cultural system dominated by a conception of the world based upon the assumption that "they simply have the right to." This is unfortunately an impoverished conception of human reason.

In liberal societies, this method of assessing whether or not an action is reasonable has traditionally been the domain of courts and tribunals, where judges have been granted the prerogative of making such rational judgements. There is a need to remove this notion from the judiciary and to make it a dominant feature of all aspects of the public sphere, in which individuals act on a daily basis with their co-citizens. This would undoubtedly imply a small cultural revolution in liberal societies, but the time may be right for it after all the lack of civicism people have seen and denounced during the Covid-19 pandemic. How can this be achieved? It has not been my intention in this book to talk about the way this new logic can be implemented. No doubt, however, state-sponsored educational systems can play a formidable role in this regard, as well as politicians, who have the potential to lead the way, as well by displaying an attitude that is no longer akin to demagogy, but rather to decisions that are taken and openly justified under the lens of practical public reason. If this logic becomes the prevalent norm in liberal societies, it will not only dramatically reframe the understanding of our actions in a way that will take into consideration the interests of the community, but also our relationship with political authority, which would then be in line with our own assessment of how we ought to behave. The day liberal societies and individuals operate according to this rationalist logic, there will no longer be a communication gap between citizens and states' reasonable requests for restraint from irresponsible behaviour when the next pandemic strikes. As a result, there will no longer be the need to impose lockdowns, strict quarantines and curfews, as is generally the case in authoritarian or totalitarian states. Liberal states have the potential to do better than the path they have followed during the Covid-19 pandemic.

Reference

Caron, Jean-François. "Rethinking the Sense of Belonging of Ethnocultural Minorities Through Reasonable Accommodations in a Liberal Perspective." *Journal of Intercultural Studies* 35, no. 6 (2014): 588–603.

PETER LANG
PROMPT

Peter Lang Prompts offer our authors the opportunity to publish original research in small volumes that are shorter and more affordable than traditional academic monographs. With a faster production time, this concise model gives scholars the chance to publish time-sensitive research, open a forum for debate, and make an impact more quickly. Like all Peter Lang publications, Prompts are thoroughly peer reviewed and can even be included in series.

For further information, please contact:

editorial@peterlang.com

To order, please contact our Customer Service Department:

peterlang@presswarehouse.com (within the U.S.)
orders@peterlang.com (outside the U.S.)

Visit our website: www.peterlang.com

Prompts include:

Claudia Aburto Guzmán, *Poesía reciente de voces en diálogo con la ascendencia hispano-hablante en los Estados Unidos: Antología breve.* ISBN 978-1-4331-5207-8. 2020

Tywan Ajani, *Barriers to Rebuilding the African American Community: Understanding the Issues Facing Today's African Americans from a Social Work Perspective.* ISBN 978-1-4331-7681-4. 2020

Macarena Areco, *Bolaño Constelaciones: Literatura, sujetos, territorios.* ISBN 978-1-4331-7575-6. 2020

Desrine Bogle. *The Transatlantic Culture Trade: Caribbean Creole Proverbs from Africa, Europe, and the Caribbean.* ISBN 978-1-4331-5723-3. 2020

Jean-François Caron. *Irresponsible Citizenship: The Cultural Roots of the Crisis of Authority in Times of Pandemic.* ISBN 978-1-4331-8908-1. 2021

Marcilio de Freitas and Marilene Corrêa da Silva Freitas, *The Future of Amazonia in Brazil: A Worldwide Tragedy.* ISBN 978-1-4331-7793-4. 2020

Mihai Dragnea. *Christian Identity Formation Across the Elbe in the Tenth and Eleventh Centuries. Christianity and Conversion in Scandinavia and the Baltic Region, c. 800–1600,* vol. 1. ISBN 978-1-4331-8431-4. 2021

Janet Farrell Leontiou, *The Doctor Still Knows Best: How Medical Culture Is Still Marked by Paternalism.* Health Communication, vol. 15. ISBN 978-1-4331-7322-6. 2020

Clare Gorman (ed.), *Miss-representation: Women, Literature, Sex and Culture.* ISBN 978-1-78874-586-4. 2020

Eva Marín Hlynsdóttir. *Gender in Organizations: The Icelandic Female Council Manager*. ISBN 978-1-4331-7729-3. 2020

Micol Kates, *Towards a Vegan-Based Ethic: Dismantling Neo-Colonial Hierarchy Through an Ethic of Lovingkindness*. ISBN 978-1-4331-7797-2. 2020

Matt Qvortrup, *Winners and Losers: Which Countries are Successful and Why?*. ISBN 978-1-80079-405-4. 2021

Peter Raina, *Doris Lessing – A Life Behind the Scenes: The Files of the British Intelligence Service MI5*. ISBN 978-1-80079-183-1. 2021

Peter Raina (trans.), *Heinrich von Kleist Poems*. ISBN 978-1-80079-043-8. 2020

Josiane Ranguin, *Mediating the Windrush Children: Caryl Phillips and Horace Ové*. ISBN 978-1-4331-7424-7. 2020

Dylan Scudder, *Coffee and Conflict in Colombia: Part of the Pentalemma Series on Managing Global Dilemmas*. ISBN 978-1-4331-7568-8. 2020

Dylan Scudder, *Conflict Minerals in the Democratic Republic of Congo: Part of the Pentalemma Series on Managing Global Dilemmas*. ISBN 978-1-4331-7561-9. 2020

Dylan Scudder, *Mining Conflict in the Philippines: Part of the Pentalemma Series on Managing Global Dilemmas*. ISBN 978-1-4331-7632-6. 2020

Dylan Scudder, *Multi-Hazard Disaster in Japan: Part of the Pentalemma Series on Managing Global Dilemmas*. ISBN 978-1-4331-7530-5. 2020

Wesley A. Stroud, *Education for Liberation, Education for Dignity: The Story of St. Monica's School of Basic Learning for Women*. ISBN 978-1-4331-7911-2. 2021

Geanneti Tavares Salomon, *Fashion and Irony in «Dom Casmurro»*. ISBN 978-1-78997-972-5. 2021

Shai Tubali, *Cosmos and Camus: Science Fiction Film and the Absurd*. ISBN 978-1-78997-664-9. 2020

Angela Williams, *Hip Hop Harem: Women, Rap and Representation in the Middle East*. ISBN 978-1-4331-7295-3. 2020

Ivan Zhavoronkov (trans.), *The Socio-Cultural and Philosophical Origins of Science* by Anatoly Nazirov. ISBN 978-1-4331-7228-1. 2020

www.ingramcontent.com/pod-product-compliance
Ingram Content Group UK Ltd.
Pitfield, Milton Keynes, MK11 3LW, UK
UKHW021822140426
5217IPUK00003B/39